The Charter School Dust-Up

Examining the Evidence on Enrollment and Achievement

◆

Martin Carnoy, Rebecca Jacobsen,
Lawrence Mishel, and Richard Rothstein

ECONOMIC POLICY INSTITUTE

About the authors

Martin Carnoy is a research associate of the Economic Policy Institute and professor of education and economics at Stanford University (carnoy@stanford.edu).

Rebecca Jacobsen is a research assistant of the Economic Policy Institute, a graduate student in politics and education at Teachers College, Columbia University, and formerly a teacher in New York City and Connecticut public schools (rjj7@columbia.edu)

Lawrence Mishel is president of the Economic Policy Institute and director of its education research and policy program (lmishel@epinet.org).

Richard Rothstein is a research associate of the Economic Policy Institute and a visiting professor at Teachers College, Columbia University (rr2159@columbia.edu).

Copyright © 2005.
Published simultaneously by the Economic Policy Institute
and Teachers College Press.

ECONOMIC POLICY INSTITUTE
1660 L Street, NW, Suite 1200
Washington, D.C. 20036
www.epinet.org

TEACHERS COLLEGE PRESS
1234 Amsterdam Avenue
New York, NY 10027
www.teacherscollegepress.com

ISBN: 0-8077-4615-0

Table of contents

Introduction and summary

In the summer of 2004, a noisy controversy erupted over whether charter schools are more effective than regular public schools. The dust-up began when the American Federation of Teachers (AFT), known to support greater restrictions on charter schools, published test results from the federal government's National Assessment of Educational Progress (NAEP). The data showed that average achievement is higher in regular public schools than in charter schools, both for students overall and for low-income students. The AFT's report also noted that for black students, a group that many charter schools are specifically designed to serve, average achievement is no better in charter schools than in regular public schools.

The *New York Times* publicized this finding on its front-page. Immediately, the most zealous advocates of charter schools responded with a storm of criticism, including a full-page advertisement that they placed in the *Times* itself. These advocates did not deny that average test scores were higher in regular public schools than in charter schools. Rather, they claimed that the AFT report was methodologically flawed because it did not attempt to compare subsets of students who were truly similar in background and prior achievement. In particular, these advocates claimed that students attending charter schools are more disadvantaged than students attending regular public schools, and especially that black students in charter schools are more disadvantaged than black students in other public schools. If this were the case, then charter school students could have been expected to score lower than regular public school students even if charter schools were somewhat more effective. These charter school advocates claimed that charter schools are actually, on average, more effective, not less so, than regular public schools.

The controversy revealed an intense level of disagreement about the wisdom of policies to encourage charter schools. That the claims are so contradictory indicates how little consensus there is about:

- whether charter schools really are more effective than public schools;

- whether charter schools really do serve comparatively disadvantaged students;

- what kind of evidence is required to make judgments about the impact of charter schools on student learning; and

- what role charter schools can be expected to play in strategies to improve regular public schools.

Our aim in this book is to synthesize as comprehensively as possible all available evidence on the average effectiveness of charter schools relative to regular public schools. We conclude in Chapter 5 that, based on 19 studies, conducted in 11 states and the District of Columbia, there is no evidence that, on average, charter schools out-perform regular public schools. In fact, there is evidence that the average impact of charter schools is negative. This evidence of a negative effect comes particularly from those studies that use the strongest methodologies to discover causal effects, although the evidence of a negative effect is somewhat localized to specific states.

In pursuing this aim, it was essential that we first set standards for methodological quality. Children are not assigned at random to attend charter schools, so some attempt must be made to identify subsets of children attending charter and regular public schools who are as similar as possible in their prior characteristics, including academic achievement. Fairly clear standards for this kind of work have emerged in social science, and we describe these in Chapter 4. We also ask whether studies adhering more or less well to these standards produce similar or different results. With few exceptions, the general outlines of the story are similar: charter schools are no more effective than regular public schools on average and may, in fact, be less effective.

But do charter schools serve more disadvantaged students than those served by regular public schools? The answer to this question is somewhat complex. In many states, the fraction of charter school students who are black is somewhat higher than the fraction of regular public school students who are black. However, the black students attending charter schools in these states tend to be disproportionately better off socioeconomically than black students attending regular public schools.

The best studies of charter school effectiveness simultaneously remove the effects not only of race and socioeconomic factors but also of prior achievement and even a host of other, often unobservable differences (such as the educational levels of parents) between children attending the two types of schools. In these highest-quality studies in particular, the average effects of attending a charter school are null or negative. In Chapter 4 we compare, in detail, the kinds of students served by charter and regular public schools nationally and in studies done in 12 states and the District of Columbia.

Beyond synthesizing current evidence, our inquiry also explores a few of the policy implications of our findings about relative average charter school performance, and this requires us to re-evaluate some of the common rationales for supporting charter schools.

One argument is that charter schools liberate educators from bureaucratic regulations and union contracts that stifle creative educational improvements. We speculate that, while deregulation helps some educators devise good schools, it also enables others to devise bad and even corruptly managed schools. For example, while some charter schools can use freedom from normal certification requirements to hire unusually talented and dedicated teachers, other charter schools use this freedom to hire teachers who may be less qualified than teachers in regular public schools. We conclude that the evidence about average charter school performance is consistent with this wide range in the effects of deregulation. That charter schools are not substantially more effective, on average, than other public schools calls into question the view that bureaucracy and union contracts are major impediments to school improvement. It seems, based on the evidence, that deregulation and deunionization do not yield any bonanzas of learning, on average. If bonanzas are realized in some places, they are apparently offset by catastrophes in others.

A second argument is that charter schools are more accountable than regular public schools for their outcomes. This theory takes two forms. Some advocates of charter schools argue that, unlike regular public schools, charter schools will be closed by public authorities if their academic performance is inadequate. We show that evidence about actual charter school accountability processes does not support this assertion. Other advocates of charter schools argue that parental choice (the freedom of parents to choose better charter schools and to remove their children from low-performing ones) provides strong accountability. We suggest that to the extent charter schools rely on this mechanism of accountability, it should not be surprising that their average academic performance does not surpass that of regular public schools, for two reasons. First, parents may choose charter schools for other than academic reasons. Second, given how complex it is to assess academic performance (leading even experts to dispute the effectiveness of charter schools so vigorously), it is not surprising that parents would not always be able to discern a charter school that was more academically effective.

A third argument is that charter schools foster experimentation to see if novel educational approaches can produce good results. We do not deny that this is an important rationale for charter schools. But we note that, in any field, a spirit of experimentation is likely to produce many failures before (if ever) identifying successes. Researchers devise strategies for widespread experimentation to discover effective practices, not to produce average gains in outcomes — those may come later, when the policies identified as effective are implemented on a large scale. Charter schools might be successful in generating innovations that should be imitated, even if average charter school test scores are at or below those of regular public schools. This implies different criteria for evaluating the merits of charter schools than the claim — that average charter school test scores surely *must* be superior — advanced by those zealous charter school advocates who were most vociferous in attacking the AFT report.

Finally, a fourth argument is that competition from charter schools improves outcomes in regular public schools because educators in regular public schools are motivated to be more effective in order to avoid losing students to charter schools. This argument for charter schools, even if valid, would not require average charter school performance to be superior to that of regular public schools. Nonetheless, we find no evidence to support the claim of a positive competition effect of charter schools, although research in this area is not yet extensive.

A potentially encouraging result from the charter school dust-up of 2004 is that the policy community may now be better able to reach consensus on what standards are appropriate for judging evidence of educational effectiveness, not only of charter schools but of regular public schools in the nation, in states, and in districts. In particular, we note that many charter school advocates criticized the AFT report for failing to (or being unable to, given data limitations) properly adjust for student background characteristics and prior test scores when evaluating charter schools. We agree with this critique. But we observe that some charter school advocates who were most vigorous in putting forward this critique have themselves been among the most outspoken opponents of making such adjustments when evaluating regular public schools and when comparing the educational effectiveness of states, schools, districts, and teachers. The dramatic change in the methodological standards of this group (detailed in Appendix A), revealed in responses to the AFT report, can increase the prospects for a more objective and fair review of public policy issues in education than we have experienced in the past. But this movement toward high methodological standards will succeed only if policy researchers apply them consistently, instead of adopting tough methodological standards only when convenient to support ideological positions. In particular, we urge that the standards set forth in the *New York Times* advertisement, placed by zealous charter school advocates in opposition to the AFT report (and reproduced in Chapter 1), be applied not only to charter school evaluation but to all school accountability policies at the federal and state levels, including those employed by the No Child Left Behind legislation.

In this book, we use two terms whose frequent repetition may be irritating to some readers. We apologize in advance for this irritation, but find it necessary nonetheless to use the terms. First, we often refer to the group of charter school advocates who have been most outspoken in their insistence that, regardless of good data, charter school performance must be superior to that of regular public schools. As one of the principal spokespersons for this group, Chester E. Finn Jr., described his and his colleagues' reaction to the AFT report: "Charter supporters rushed to the barricades after last week's AFT-coordinated blast in the *New York Times*." For want of a better term, we call this group of barricade-rushers "charter school zealots." We intend no disrespect to this group, and use "zealot" as Webster's dictionary defines it: "someone who acts for a cause with excessive zeal (persistent, fervent devotion)." It is necessary to use a term for members of this group to distinguish them from many other supporters of charter schools whose devotion to charter schools is not excessive and who did not rush to the barricades following the release of the AFT's report. Supporters of charter schools may have many reasons for their support, and these reasons do not require an *a priori* belief that average charter school academic performance must be superior to that of regular public schools. These reasons might include beliefs that charter schools are a way to keep parents committed to public education by offering them more choice, a way to work around some or all of the administrative and union constraints that characterize many regular public schools, a way to keep some children in school who might otherwise be "lost," or a way to involve parents more actively in decisions about their children's education.

It is not the purpose of this book to evaluate in any depth the merits of these reasons for supporting charter schools or to propose policies regarding charter schools. We do, however, observe that any policy that permits parents to choose schools other than their neighborhood schools can involve costs as well as benefits, and that the difficult trade-offs involved in school choice have been too little discussed. For example, we note that if more academically able children exit their regular public schools in favor of charter schools (or, in the regular public sector, in favor of magnet or exam schools), this makes the task of neighborhood public schools more difficult because the students who remain will, on average, be less academically able and will lose the benefit of interaction with their more academically able peers. We also note that some evidence indicates that the existence of charter schools increases racial segregation in public schooling. These are not reasons to reject charter schooling, but policy deliberations must weigh these against the benefits claimed by charter school supporters.

There are also zealots who oppose charter schools. In this book, we aim to be fair and accurate, but we do not attempt to achieve an artificial "balance" by analyzing the zealotry of charter school opponents as well. Charter school zealots, for example, accuse the AFT of opposing charter schools at least partly because they threaten the union's institutional interests. In examining the accuracy of the data analysis of NAEP charter school scores presented by the AFT, we do not find a need to examine the interests that may have motivated the AFT to perform this accurate analysis. Militant and unreflective charter school opposition, by the AFT or other influential policy makers, was not prominent in the dust-up following the AFT's report, and it is this controversy, and only this controversy, whose implications this book examines.

The other term we use repetitively is "on average" to describe data about charter and regular public schools. Without such a term, many readers may still appreciate that when data comparisons of charter and regular public schools are made, only averages are being described — there can be wide variation of achievement within a particular school (whether it is a charter or a regular public school), and there can be wide variation in the average achievement of schools that are charter schools and of schools that are regular public schools. But some readers may benefit from a reminder that a conclusion that charter school performance lags behind that of regular public school performance is not inconsistent with an observation that many charter schools may be far superior to typical regular public schools (and some may be greatly inferior). Or, typical charter schools may be superior to many regular public schools. Unfortunately, good data on school performance are so limited that we have almost no understanding of the variance of mean charter school academic achievement or of the variance of mean regular public school achievement. NAEP could not report such data, because NAEP reports test scores only of students, not of individual schools. And the state studies we examine, although they collect data on school mean performance levels, do not report standard deviations of these school means of performance, a statistic that would be needed to understand the extent to which average performance in charter schools is typical for charter schools generally. Because this is such a critical point, we keep it before the reader by frequently inserting the words "on average" in our discussion.

The co authors of this book are not opponents, zealous or otherwise, of charter schools; among ourselves, we have a variety of ways in which we balance the costs and benefits of charter schools. The message of this book is not that charter schools have "failed," but only that there is no reason to be surprised that their average performance apparently falls below that of regular public schools. We believe that a more reasoned discussion of education policy can proceed from this recognition.

CHAPTER 1

The reaction to the AFT's report on charter school scores

Using NAEP data available to the public on the website of the National Center for Education Statistics (NCES), but not yet published by NCES in a summary document, researchers at the American Federation of Teachers published, in August 2004, an analysis of these data showing that, overall, charter school students had test scores that were a full half a grade lower than scores of students in regular public schools (AFT 2004a). The AFT further showed that the test performance of black charter school students was about the same as that of black students in regular public schools, but for students in central cities and for those with lunch eligibility,[1] charter school test performance was worse than regular public school test performance.

Prior to its own publication, the AFT made its findings available to Diana Jean Schemo, an education reporter for the *New York Times*, who published an article headlined, "Nation's Charter Schools Lagging Behind, U.S. Test Scores Reveal." The article said that NAEP data showed "charter school students often doing worse than comparable students in regular public schools," and that charter schools did no better than regular public schools with black, low-income, and inner-city children (Schemo 2004).

Because charter schools have been promoted by many charter school supporters as a way to lift academic achievement (particularly for disadvantaged students) above the level reached in regular public schools, the AFT's analysis was, at first glance, surprising. No commentators, including those who advocate charter and private schools as alternatives to regular public education, denied that the AFT analysis accurately reflected the NAEP data. Indeed, as we show below, the NCES subsequently issued its own analysis (NAEP 2005) of the NAEP data that confirmed, in its essential findings, the AFT's conclusions. But many charter school advocates took strong exception to any inference that NAEP data might suggest that charter schools could be ineffective because their students' achievement is lower. These commentators found such a suggestion in the AFT report and in the *Times* article, and condemned both.

As Chester E. Finn Jr., a prominent charter school proponent wrote, "Charter supporters rushed to the barricades after last week's AFT-coordinated blast in the *New York Times*" (Finn 2004c). Indeed, there was a blizzard of harsh responses to the AFT report and to the *Times'* coverage of it. Throughout the fall of 2004, supporters of charter schools published, in print and on the web, critiques of the AFT's report and arguments about why conclusions regarding charter school effectiveness, based on that report, should be dismissed.

On August 18, the day following the *Times* article, William G. Howell, Paul E. Peterson, and Martin R. West, political scientists who are prominent students of and advocates for school vouchers, published a *Wall Street Journal* op-ed essay, "Dog Eats AFT Homework," denouncing the AFT report (Howell, Peterson, and West 2004). The next day, the Reverend Floyd H. Flake, a former congressman and president of Edison Charter Schools (a private firm that contracts with public school districts to operate schools as charter schools), published a similar op-ed in the *New York Times* itself (Flake 2004).

A week later, a group of charter school supporters and social scientists took out a full-page advertisement in the *Times*. The signers, many of whom have written favorably about vouchers, charter schools, and other forms of school choice, said in the advertisement that they were "dismayed by the prominent, largely uncritical coverage given by *The New York Times* to a study of charter schools by the American Federation of Teachers" (CER 2004a). **Exhibit A** reproduces the text of the advertisement.[2] The sponsor of the advertisement, the Center for Education Reform, and its president, Jeanne Allen, circulated additional attacks on the AFT report on the center's website (CER 2004b).

The Education Leaders Council, an organization of conservative education officials founded by former Arizona state schools superintendent Lisa Graham Keegan, published a similar denunciation of what it termed the AFT's "misinformation" (ELC 2004). Andrew Rotherham, director of the Progressive Policy Institute's education program and another charter school advocate, wrote that the AFT report was a "hatchet

Exhibit A - Text of advertisement by the Center for Education Reform in the *New York Times*, August 25, 2004

Charter School Evaluation Reported by *The New York Times* Fails to Meet Professional Standards

We, the undersigned members of the research community, are dismayed by the prominent, largely uncritical coverage given by *The New York Times* to a study of charter schools by the American Federation of Teachers (AFT). According to the paper's lead news story on August 17, the analysis shows "charter school students often doing worse than comparable students in regular public schools."

The study in question does not meet current professional research standards. As a result, it tells us nothing about whether charter schools are succeeding. The following considerations are key:

■ **Data Quality.** The study is based on data from the 2003 National Assessment of Educational Progress (NAEP). Often referred to as the Nation's Report Card, NAEP provides a valuable snapshot of student performance nationwide at a single point in time. But since only limited family background information is currently available for the 2003 NAEP, the study does not provide reliable information on the effectiveness of any particular type of school.

■ **Only One Set of Test Scores.** Because only one year of information is available for charter schools from NAEP, the study provides test scores for only one point in time. But without better background information, accurately measuring school effectiveness requires information on student performance from at least two points in time.

■ **Limited Background Information.** Because of limited NAEP information on family background, the study does not take into account such key characteristics of students known to affect their performance as parental education, household income, and the quality of learning resources in the home.

■ **Unsophisticated Analysis.** When analyzing charter schools' effects on student performance, the study considers differences in only one family background characteristic at a time. To obtain accurate estimates, all available background characteristics must be considered simultaneously.

■ **What NAEP *Can* Tell Us.** NAEP data do show that charter schools tend to serve a relatively disadvantaged population. As compared with traditional public schools, a higher proportion of students in charter schools are eligible for the federal free or reduced price lunch program, are from minority backgrounds, and attend a school located in a central city.

■ **Journalistic Responsibility.** The news media has an obligation to assess carefully any research sponsored by interest groups engaged in policy de-

(continued on the next page)

**Exhibit A - Text of advertisement by the Center for Education
Reform in the *New York Times*, August 25, 2004
(continued)**

bates. Such studies need to be vetted by independent scholars, as is commonly
done in coverage of research on the biological and physical sciences.

■ **Further Research.** To date, we lack definitive evidence on the effectiveness of
charter schools, in part because they are so new and so varied. Fortunately, higher-
quality research on charter schools is already underway. Still more needs to be
done before jumping to conclusions about the merits of one of the nation's most
prominent education reform strategies.

Julian R. Betts, University of California, San Diego
John E. Brandl, University of Minnesota
David E. Campbell, University of Notre Dame
Mary Beth Celio, University of Washington
James G. Cibulka, University of Kentucky
Gregory U. Cizek, University of North Carolina, Chapel Hill
David N. Figlio, University of Florida
David J. Francis, University of Houston
Howard L. Fuller, Marquette University
Charles Glenn, Boston University
Jay P. Greene, Manhattan Institute
Eric A. Hanushek, Stanford University
James J. Heckman, University of Chicago
Paul T. Hill, University of Washington
William G. Howell, Harvard University
Caroline M. Hoxby, Harvard University
Tom Loveless, The Brookings Institution
Robert Maranto, Villanova University
Terry M. Moe, Stanford University
Thomas J. Nechyba, Duke University
Paul E. Peterson, Harvard University
Michael Podgursky, University of Missouri, Columbia
Margaret E. Raymond, Stanford University
Jonah Rockoff, Columbia University
Simeon Slovacek, California State University, Los Angeles
Tim R. Sass, Florida State University
Paul Teske, University of Colorado, Denver
Richard K. Vedder, Ohio University
Herbert J. Walberg, University of Illinois, Chicago
Martin R. West, Harvard University
Patrick J. Wolf, Georgetown University

This ad was sponsored by The Center for Education Reform.

job" (Rotherham 2004a). Caroline Hoxby, a professor of economics at Harvard, told the *Harvard Education Letter* that the AFT report was "the worst study I have ever seen on charter schools" (Rothman 2004a).

Howard Fuller, chairman of the Charter School Leadership Council, a coalition of charter school advocacy groups, issued a statement calling the Schemo article in the *New York Times* "misleading" and added (despite the undisputed accuracy of the NAEP data) that "[r]eaders should bear in mind the adage, 'consider the source': the data used by the *Times* was provided by a national teachers union long opposed to charter schools" (Fuller 2004a). In a subsequent statement, the Charter School Leadership Council claimed that the AFT had a "conflict of interest" in reporting on the NAEP data, because its lobbyists had participated in an effort to "block the passage of, or at least water down" legislation that would have made it easier to establish charter schools, and has been "fighting the charter movement" in other ways (CSLC 2004).

The Bush Administration, which promotes charter schools as alternatives to regular public schools, also weighed in. In response to the *Times'* article, Robert Lerner, commissioner of the National Center for Education Statistics, wrote a letter to the *Times* saying that "[m]any factors affect student achievement, including socioeconomic status, race and ethnicity and prior test scores. The current database does not account for these factors simultaneously. A more thorough analysis is needed to provide a statistically sound report, and we are working on one [for charter schools]" (Lerner 2004).[3]

These charter school advocates claimed that comparing NAEP scores of charter and regular public school fourth-graders is a misleading basis on which to judge whether charter schools outperform regular public schools. They argued that the charter school data suffer from an inability to control for relevant predictors of student performance, particularly related to the social and economic disadvantages of many charter school students: because these students may come from families with severe disadvantages, it is understandable that charter school students' scores would be lower.

Some zealous charter school advocates explained the AFT's finding — that black, low income, and central city students did no better in charter schools — by asserting that charter school students may be even more disadvantaged than typical black, low-income, or central city students. As Martin R. West put it in a written statement to the *Washington*

Post, "black students who attend charter schools may well come from poorer families than black students in traditional public schools" (Mathews 2004). Further, some charter school supporters claimed that the NAEP analysis had a bias that was even more subtle, unrelated to the potentially measurable economic conditions that charter school students and their parents experience. For example, they said, charter schools may attract students whose family characteristics are similar to those of public school students, but who are having greater academic difficulties in public schools. Families may enroll their children in charter schools specifically because they are already not doing as well as their classmates. If charter schools select the lowest-performing students, their average performance would still be low, even with greater gains. As charter school advocates William G. Howell and Martin R. West (2005) put it:

> As schools of choice, charters are likely to attract students who are not doing well in their traditional public schools. Moreover, many charter schools explicitly target "at-risk" students. Both of these facts would lead you to expect students in charter schools to perform at a low level even after taking into account their observable background characteristics.

Or as Jeanne Allen and the Center for Education Reform stated on the group's website, "NAEP data puts charter schools in the same box as traditional public schools — not taking into account the fact that many charter students enter the classroom two to three grade levels below average" (CER 2004c). And John Chubb, chief education officer of the Edison Schools (2004) responded to the report by stating, "It is unfortunate, though entirely predictable, that the AFT, an organization on record for more than two years for the need for a moratorium on charter schools, would stoop so low as to brand schools guilty of little else than working with low-achieving students."

The only accurate way to judge the relative performance of charter and regular public school students, these charter school zealots said, was to assess the same students at two different times, so that gains students made from grade to grade can be compared. As the *Times* advertisement said, "accurately measuring school effectiveness requires information on student performance from at least two points in time."

If, for example, charter school third-graders made greater gains in achievement by the time they reached the fourth grade than regular public school third-graders made in the same year, then charter schools could be superior even if, because their third-graders started at a lower level, the charter school fourth grade scores were still lower than regular public school fourth grade scores.

In their attacks on the AFT report and *Times* article, some charter school advocates also dismissed comparisons based on NAEP scores because, they said, many charter schools are new and it takes time for a new school to become stable enough to prove the competence of its staff and its instructional approach. Howell and West (2005) claimed that the AFT had "hoodwinked" the *Times,* partly because

> [h]aving just hired new staff and teachers, implemented new curricula, and acquired building facilities, new schools often face considerable start-up problems. Almost one-third of the charter schools nationwide were less than two years old when the NAEP was administered....

It is unfair, these critics argued, to judge such schools by their scores at a time when kinks are first being worked out of their methods, and when students, teachers, and administrators are first getting accustomed to working together. Charter schools, these supporters suggest, need time before their test scores should be taken too seriously, or before they should be held accountable for academic performance. In response to the AFT's report, Mark Cannon, executive director of the National Association of Charter School Authorizers (NACSA), released this statement (2004):

> Research indicates that charters school students show more growth over time than their counterparts in traditional public schools. Part of the answer lies in how the charter school itself matures after its first 2 or 3 years of operation. Most charter schools are start-up entities, and they perform better after having time to build a cohesive school community and work through the formidable challenge of starting a new public school with less funding than traditional schools receive and usually without any support for a facility.
>
> For valid and meaningful evaluation, it makes sense to give charter schools 3 years to become established, especially knowing that they

will be held to account for their results typically within another 2 years (given that the average charter term is set at 5 years).

Indeed, all education research and policy making could benefit from such wisdom. No prescription for school improvement should be evaluated before sufficient time has passed for the treatment to mature, as well as for initial "Hawthorne effects" to dissipate.[4]

CHAPTER 2

Can the 'dust-up' lead to a new consensus in education research and policy?

Both the AFT and the *New York Times* invited some of these attacks by over-interpreting the NAEP data. The AFT's website summarizes its report with the headline, "Charter Schools Underperforming," a conclusion that the charter school zealots properly noted cannot be sustained on the basis of a single year of NAEP scores (AFT 2004b). The AFT report showed that regular public school students had higher test scores than charter school students in both reading and math, differences which were statistically significant. However, test scores by race showed no statistically significant differences between charter and other public school scores. The report did show a statistically significant regular public school advantage in test scores for some other subgroups: among students in the central city and among low-income students (those with lunch eligibility). The report also showed that, with or without tests for statistical significance, there was only one case where charter school students had higher achievement than comparable public school students — among rural/small town students. The *Times* article exaggerated these very small regular public school advantages when it said that charter school students "often" do worse than "comparable" students in regular public schools.

Yet heated though this controversy over charter school NAEP results might have been, it can play an important role in how we frame future discussions about American school performance. Indeed, the standards set forth in the Center for Education Reform's *New York Times* advertisement (Exhibit A) should guide standards for evaluating any claims about school performance, whether regular public, private, or charter.

A new consensus, emerging from the charter school controversy, should include these agreements:

- Student and family characteristics matter in evaluating school performance. One cannot properly interpret test scores without keeping in mind the characteristics of the school population those scores describe. Children's family, economic, social, and racial advantages and disadvantages, as well as school quality, affect where students start, how much progress they make, and where they end up at the time of testing. School quality cannot be inferred from comparisons of the test score levels of children whose background characteristics differ.

- Student background characteristics are complex, and cannot be described simply by noting students' race or ethnicity or whether their family incomes fall below 185% of the national poverty line (the cut-off for lunch eligibility). For fair and meaningful school accountability to be possible, the nation and states require a more comprehensive student data system that includes items like parental education levels, while preserving student privacy.

- Changes in test scores are meaningful only insofar as the same students are observed. If we want to know how much children are learning, or how much more they are learning than other children, we need data over time for the same children. Comparing scores of children in the same grade in different years cannot tell us if a school is improving, because the average characteristics of the children in a particular grade can change from year to year even if the children seem, based on their race or lunch eligibility, to be similar. Care even needs to be exercised in trying to follow a particular group of students, because some schools have very high student turnover (mobility), so this year's fourth-graders may not be the same children as last year's third-graders. Annual "progress" can only meaningfully refer to how much a specific group of children learns from the third to the fourth grade; it cannot meaningfully refer to how much more or less one group of fourth-graders knows compared to another group.

However, even this approach may be over-simplified. Although score gains of a single cohort of students over time are a more accurate indicator of school effectiveness than single point-in-time score levels, they are still not fully accurate and should not, therefore, be relied upon exclusively to evaluate the quality of a school (Raudenbush 2004). Because students whose previous scores are at different levels may not have equal difficulty making gains, even an apparent difference in gain scores may not indicate charter school success or failure, if charter schools truly do enroll students who have lower initial scores (Ladd and Walsh 2002; Ballou 2002).[5]

Whether it is the case that students who start lower can more easily (or with greater difficulty) make gains, NAEP provides no data on gains made by students as they progress from third to fourth grade, so NAEP fourth-grade scores cannot conclusively indicate whether charter or regular public schools are superior.[6] Although gain scores are not, by themselves, a fully sufficient measure of school effectiveness, the zealous charter school advocates, in their criticism of drawing inferences from NAEP data, were correct that gain scores are more informative than point-in-time score levels.

• Even if we accept gain scores as a more accurate measure than point-in-time score levels of school effectiveness, gains of children in different sets of schools (regular public compared to charter, for example), may not be fairly comparable because the children may differ in ways that are difficult for researchers to observe. For example, particular schools may disproportionately attract students with less motivation or self-discipline, or with unmeasured family and community characteristics that affect their likelihood of success in school. Thus, school effects can easily be overestimated, even when gain scores are used, if these "unobservables" are not dealt with in one of a number of ways that researchers now use to account for possible "selection bias."[7]

If this consensus holds, then its policy implications go beyond how we evaluate charter schools. It should lead to a consensus that federal and state education policies — expressed, for example, in the federal "No Child Left Behind" (NCLB) law — should be dramatically over-hauled. The present law makes judgments of school improvement by comparing test scores in a particular grade in consecutive years. This is a comparison of different students.[8] Further, schools are evaluated based on measuring how many students achieve a given standard of proficiency, but if family characteristics influence student performance, then it must be harder for some schools to reach proficiency than others. While identifying standards that we want children to meet can be helpful, eliminating achievement gaps between low-income, minority, immigrant, and other students may not be possible for schools to accomplish on their own if student characteristics affect test scores.[9] While exhortations for all schools to reach proficiency are meant to inspire greater efforts, if goals are set that are impossible to meet, the result can be disillusionment, deflated morale, and the loss of public support for schools that may be doing a good job. Just as charter school supporters feared that an overly simplified account of student test scores could lead to a loss of support for charter schools, so can such an overly simplified account undermine public support for regular public schools.[10]

CHAPTER 3

Problems with the critiques of the NAEP report by charter school supporters

No schools, charter or regular public, should be evaluated using point-in-time score levels

The charter school zealots were on solid ground in complaining about conclusions that charter schools are not succeeding, when these conclusions are based solely on a single year of data from NAEP. Comparisons of score levels between schools may provide misleading information about the relative performance of these schools if accurate data about gains are not also available and the characteristics of students are not adequately taken into account.

The zealots were also correct that the demographic categories used by NAEP (and by almost all other standardized tests) are much too broad to permit accurate comparisons of students. "Low-income" students, for example, identified by lunch eligibility, include children from homeless families with little or no cash income, as well as children from stable lower-middle-class families with two parents and two children and with income as high as $35,000 a year. A school with a large proportion of homeless children could have lower test scores than a school with a large proportion of lower-middle-class children, but the former could still be a better school if its gain scores were more significant. If, as the zealous charter school advocates suggested, "low-income" charter schools typically enroll higher proportions of the extremely poor or disadvantaged, while "low-income" regular public schools typically enroll higher proportions of lower-middle-class children (who, despite their higher family income, are still lunch-eligible), then NAEP comparisons could mask a superiority of charter schools. Likewise, if charter schools typically enroll black students who are more "at-risk" than typical black students, the effectiveness of charter schools could also be masked by comparing NAEP scores of blacks in charter and in regular public schools.

The zealous charter school advocates are also correct that it does a disservice to judge a school's results by its test scores if that school is unstable. Some schools, in very low-income neighborhoods, have extraordinarily high pupil mobility, making it difficult to raise student achievement for their very transient students. As rents in urban neighborhoods escalate more rapidly than low-wage workers' incomes, families tend to move more frequently and to transfer their children from school to school. Indeed, one recent study of schools in Texas found that, if black students' families moved no more frequently than white students' families, one-seventh of the test score gap between black and white students would be eliminated by a change in this single socioeconomic variable (Hanushek, Kain, and Rivkin 2004). Some schools in urban areas have student mobility rates of well over 100% annually, harming students psychologically and socially, as well as academically (GAO 1994; Kerbow 1996; Bruno and Isken 1996; Rumberger et al. 1999). It is impossible to make judgments about the effectiveness of schools that experience high rates of student turnover that are beyond these schools' control. If charter schools serving minority and low-income students typically have less stability, either because they are new or because students' families move more frequently than families of students in regular public schools, then NAEP comparisons could in this way as well mask a superiority of charter schools.

However, some student mobility is within schools' control. This is mobility not due to family residential moves but due to schools' inability to hold the allegiance of students when choice is available. In addition, some schools are unstable not because they were recently founded but because they may be experimenting with new instructional programs or may have a new principal or a high turnover of teachers. Comparisons of school effectiveness should also evaluate these characteristics, which are not captured by NAEP or other test scores.

For these and similar reasons, the zealots' insistence was appropriate that no definitive inference about relative charter school quality should be drawn from the AFT's report of NAEP data.[11] However, these advocates' position is inconsistent with how they have typically commented about regular public schools. Indeed, much of their support for charter schools is based on an assessment of public school failure that uses the very reasoning that they have denounced when applied to charter schools. Some charter school advocates have been outspoken and uncompromising critics of regular public schools' performance, especially for disadvantaged children.

There is a contradiction between zealous charter school advocates' previous condemnation of the performance of regular public schools and their current outrage that observers might use the same kind of evidence to criticize charter schools. Many of these charter school advocates have typically been quick, as well, to denounce any suggestion that public schools with unusually disadvantaged children may be doing a good job despite having low score levels.

Shortcomings of 'No Child Left Behind' performance measures

Next, we turn to the contradiction between standards for evaluating charter school performance articulated by charter school zealots and the standards for performance embedded in the Bush Administration's "No Child Left Behind" law.

We don't intend to exaggerate the inconsistency in charter school zealots' positions. Some of them acknowledge the limitations of standardized test score levels as adequate definitions of school performance, and have advocated holding schools accountable for the year-to-year gains of individual students as well as for the levels of achievement that schools produce.

For example, a vocal critic of the AFT's report on charter school NAEP results, Chester E. Finn Jr., recently published (with Frederick M. Hess) a compelling indictment of the use of point-in-time rather than gain scores in the NCLB accountability system (Finn and Hess 2004). They forthrightly call for revision of the NCLB law, arguing that:

> Adequate yearly progress [the NCLB standard] should be gauged based primarily on the academic value schools add (that is, the achievement gains their pupils make) — not, as is the case today, on the aggregate level at which students perform. Measuring a student's overall level of achievement encompasses three things — learning in

the current school year, learning in all previous years, and everything else going on in the child's life — of which only the first is relevant to gauging whether schools and educators are performing adequately....[U]nder a "value-added" system, a student is tested at the beginning of fourth grade and again at the end of the year...a terrific way of evaluating teacher and school effectiveness that largely washes out the influence of children's backgrounds and prior attainment. Today's NCLB is hostile to value-added analysis. That should change.[12]

As we noted above, gain scores do not entirely "wash out" the influence of children's backgrounds and prior attainment, so an accountability system that relies too rigidly on such scores can still be subject to abuse. Nonetheless, reforming NCLB accountability to set standards for gains, not levels, would be an enormous improvement.

However, despite such acknowledgments of the limitations of test score levels, many charter school advocates still consider these limitations to be only a minor problem for the evaluation of regular public schools, a problem not serious enough to cause them to withdraw their support for accountability systems, at the state and national levels, that condemn regular public schools as failing based on low test score levels, irrespective of students' backgrounds or their prior achievement. Indeed, much of the advocacy for charter schools as an alternative is based on claims that almost all regular public schools serving the most disadvantaged children are failing, based on evidence of the type that zealous charter school advocates now dismiss.[13] Charter school advocates who were the most severe critics of the AFT's charter school NAEP report have not directed similar vitriol toward state and national test-score-based accountability systems whose flaws are similar to those of NAEP-based judgments of charter school effectiveness.

Despite some misgivings about the overuse of standardized tests, many charter school zealots have been aggressive proponents of the Bush Administration's No Child Left Behind law and its strict sanctions for regular public schools. If, as these charter school proponents insisted in response to the AFT's NAEP report, school test scores do not reflect school performance without adequately accounting for student characteristics, then, it would seem to follow, that a substantial revision of NCLB accountability measures is needed. Consider, for instance, the measure of "adequate yearly progress" in NCLB: proficiency levels of students in a particular grade are compared to the proficiency levels of a different group of students who were in that grade in an earlier year.

NCLB also offers insufficient exemption from its penalties to schools with high student turnover, whether because of unavoidable student mobility or because schools are having start-up problems or are in transition with new staff or instructional programs.[14] If there are start-up or transition problems for charter schools that limit their academic performance, then perhaps there ought to be an exemption from NCLB for regular schools undergoing transitions. If it makes sense to give charter schools an opportunity to stabilize before their test scores are taken as indicative of school quality, then regular public schools should perhaps also be eligible for a three-year exemption from accountability when a new principal takes over or a new instructional program is adopted. Similarly, accountability measures in NCLB ought to take into account that some schools have very unstable student populations. This is a serious matter to address in any effort to hold schools in disadvantaged communities accountable based on test scores: there is often a very large turnover of the student population each year in these schools, and so the particular test scores of an individual school may not reflect the extent to which the performance of students has actually benefited or been harmed by the quality of the school's instruction.

How charter school zealots helped create the NAEP charter sample

It is indicative of the inconsistency in the positions of zealous charter school advocates that those who now insist that point-in-time NAEP scores are inappropriate to use for comparisons of charter and regular public schools are the same advocates who, in 2002, pressed the National Assessment Governing Board (the federal agency that oversees the NAEP) to create the data that the AFT analyzed: a nationally representative sample of charter schools in the 2003 reading and math NAEP exams. At the time, these charter school advocates apparently expected to use NAEP to compare the achievement of students in charter and regular public schools to confirm their expectation that charter school scores would be higher. The proposal to include a nationally representative sample of charter schools in the next NAEP administration was made by Governing Board member Chester E. Finn Jr. on behalf of the Charter School Leadership Council, which he described as "a loose coalition of groups that support charter schools" that sought "national data on the academic achievement of their students" (NAGB 2002). Mr. Finn (2004a) says that he was joined in this proposal by Lisa Keegan, then-president of the Education Leaders Council that, as noted above, publicly attacked the AFT report. In addition to Mr. Finn's Thomas B. Fordham Foundation and Ms. Keegan's Education Leaders Council, the Charter School Leadership Council included the Progressive Policy Institute (PPI) and the Black Alliance for Educational Options (BAEO), whose leaders have also now dismissed the validity of the NAEP scores they initially requested. Mr. Finn says that the group's proposal to include a charter school sample in NAEP was based mainly on "an instinct: there are schools, we care about how they're doing, we need to know how their kids are doing, and it's been bloody hard to get comparable data from other sources" (Finn 2004e). Yet upon the AFT's release of the NAEP results, Mr. Finn himself called the report a "mischief-bearing grenade" that "defamed" charter schools, partly because:

> [W]hen judging a school, one ought not settle for absolute test scores alone. What one most wants to know about a school is how rapidly its pupils are making progress from wherever they started, i.e., how much academic value is the school itself adding. You can't determine that from NAEP data. (Finn 2004b.)

Mr. Finn was, of course, right about the limitations of NAEP data, but one wonders why, then, he pressed the government to collect these data on charter school test scores in the first place. In 2002, he apparently believed they were "comparable." Mr. Finn had previously been chairman of the National Assessment Governing Board that oversees NAEP, so it was no surprise to him that NAEP has never been designed to detect how much academic value a school or group of schools is adding. In now condemning the AFT's NAEP report, Mr. Finn was holding the AFT study to a standard that he knew it could not meet, even though he urged the collection of the data for what could only have been a study with these limitations.

Indeed, according to the *Times* article, as a member of the Governing Board, Mr. Finn had previously opposed restricting NAEP analyses of regular public schools to those that controlled for student characteristics, arguing that such a restriction "would compromise the credibility of the assessment results by trying to blame demographic and other outside factors for poor performance" (Schemo 2004).[15]

Similar inconsistencies characterized many of the public statements by other charter school advocates following the release of the NAEP data that they, themselves, had demanded. We provide prominent examples of these inconsistencies in Appendix A, including reviews of current and previous statements of charter school zealots, such as former NCES Commissioner Robert Lerner, former U.S. Secretary of Education Rodney Paige, Jeanne Allen and the Center for Education Reform, the Rev. Floyd Flake, Jay Greene, the Black Alliance for Educational Options, and Howard Fuller.

We present this Appendix not in an attempt to embarrass zealous charter school advocates by highlighting their inconsistencies but rather to challenge them to conform their views on the evaluation of charter and regular public schools to a consistent standard.

Consistency can be achieved, we suggest, in either of two ways:

- Point-in-time score levels, controlled only for race, ethnicity, and lunch eligibility. These are one way to judge school effectiveness in both the regular public and charter school sectors, using a common standard. However, we do not endorse this approach to consistency and hope that charter school zealots will not do so either, because it is a flawed way to evaluate schools for all the reasons upon which these advocates insisted when the AFT's NAEP report was issued.

- Evaluation of schools, charter and regular public, with more sophisticated demographic controls than are usually available and with controls for the prior performance of specific student cohorts. We endorse this approach, but note that it demands a radical overhaul of school accountability policies now embedded in federal and state law.

CHAPTER 4

Are charter school students more disadvantaged than regular public school students, and does this explain charter schools' unexpectedly low NAEP scores?

How selection bias complicates the evaluation of charter schools

In the first section of this report, we noted the charter school proponents' claim that comparisons of fourth-grade regular public and charter school NAEP scores are invalid because charter schools serve more disadvantaged children, even if the students seem superficially similar in race and in socioeconomic status. In other words, the academic performance of black students in charter schools cannot be appropriately compared with the performance of black students in regular public schools because black students in charter schools are more disadvantaged than black students in regular public schools, and black students enter charter schools with lower scores than black students who remain in regular public schools.

As noted above, we agree with the charter school zealots that a comparison of gains made by students who are truly similar in their social and economic characteristics, and in their prior test scores, would be the only fair way to compare school types. Data from charter schools may suffer from "selection bias" if low-income students who enter charter schools are not demographically or academically typical of all low-income students.

In this section of the report, we examine whether, in fact, charter school students typically are more disadvantaged than regular public school students in similar demographic categories. Several charter school advocates have asserted that this is the case, but have provided no evidence to support this claim. They have said that charter schools enroll more black and more low-income students than do regular public schools nationwide, but if charter schools provided superior education, this would not explain why test scores for black (or low-income) students are no higher in charter schools than test scores of black (or low-income) students in regular public schools. These charter school advocates have offered a few anecdotal accounts of charter schools that enroll unusually disadvantaged children from within the broad demographic categories of "black" and "low income," but have not shown that such cases are typical.

If charter school students are, in fact, more disadvantaged than regular public school students in similar demographic categories, then point-in-time comparisons of NAEP data would not adequately reflect the contributions of charter schools. But if charter school students, on the whole, are less disadvantaged than regular public school students in similar demographic categories, then conclusions from the NAEP data that charter school performance is inadequate would be more plausible.

Charter schools may have enrolled particularly disadvantaged students in cases where the schools were created primarily to correct "mismanaged" public schools, or when private companies were brought in by school district officials to "turn around" schools in which students were performing more poorly than demographically similar students in other schools in the same district. There is little doubt that some charter schools are granted charters precisely to attack the problem of lower-scoring students. For example, management organizations such as Edison Schools have established charter schools at the invitation of public school districts to try to improve student performance in historically low-performing schools. Some of the most vociferous charter school advocates who objected to the AFT's NAEP report have close ties to Edison, and their views may be influenced by this experience.[16] But while in some districts Edison may serve students who were initially performing more poorly than demographically comparable students, Edison schools are a small minority of all charter schools nationwide, and even a small minority of all charter schools that serve black and Hispanic children. So it is not evident if, overall, charter schools serve children who are more at risk than demographically comparable children, or if they do so to a great enough extent that this could explain the nationally representative NAEP data. If charter schools did typically serve more at-risk students, then it would be a badge of superior accomplishment that charter school student scores were identical to regular school student scores, after controlling for race and income.

Yet it is also plausible that selection bias of the opposite type occurs. Charter schools may have more flexibility than regular public schools to pick their students, so they may be able to deny admission to potentially troublesome students. Although charter schools that have a surplus of applicants may choose the successful applicants by lottery, this will not ensure a representative student body if the applicant pool is not representative. Again, there are anecdotal accounts of such practices, documented, for example, in a study of charter schools in California (Wells et al. 1998) and in a description of an Edison charter school in Boston (Farber 1998). Below, we also discuss how such selection bias affects the student population at KIPP schools. Charter schools may also appeal to the most motivated parents, eager to provide opportunities for their children that they feel are lacking in regular public schools, and more inclined (or able) to offer ongoing support for learning that is critical for academic success. Thus, while the zealous charter school advocates are correct that the NAEP data may understate the effectiveness of charter schools, it is also possible that the NAEP data may overstate their effectiveness, if charter schools enroll children who are more advantaged relative to their broad demographic groupings.

The only nearly foolproof way to correct for selection bias and determine whether charter and regular public school students are truly similar in their potential would be to do an experiment. Students could be randomly assigned to charter schools and regular public schools, and their performance compared for several years. Because charter schools are schools of choice, and their claims of effectiveness rest partly on the fact that students choose to attend, the random assignment pool would have to consist of regular public school students who wanted to attend charter schools, some of whom were randomly offered admission and others of whom were not. Experimental results would be most reliable if students who were offered admission actually attended the charter school, while students who were denied admission attended their regular public schools (rather than choose another charter school). Yet even if carried out flawlessly, the results of such experiments would still suffer from problems of generalizability (the difficulty of reproducing the treatment on a larger scale), if they were interpreted as having implications for charter and regular public schools generally. That is because both the experimental and control groups would consist of students (or parents) who were motivated enough to try to choose such charter schools, a characteristic that would not be common to all regular public school students (or parents). The experiments could indicate, however, whether charter schools were more effective than regular public schools for the sub-population of more motivated students and parents. Nonetheless, such experiments are expensive to carry out, do not always result in unbiased estimates if participants leave the experiment in large numbers or non-randomly, and cannot realistically be performed unless there is a shortage of charter school spaces beyond the control of the experiment and a surplus of applicants.[17]

Short of such experiments, researchers can try to simulate an experimental situation by adjusting student performance for a greater number of measurable variables, known to influence test scores, than are usually accounted for in data like the NAEP. For example, beyond comparisons based on race and ethnicity, lunch eligibility, and central city residence that the AFT was able to control for in its NAEP analysis (and, given the capacities of the NAEP data tool available to the public, only able to control for each separately), researchers could also control for multiple backgrounds simultaneously or add controls for background factors such as language spoken at home, parents' education, gradations of family income, parents' motivation, student mobility between schools, and community environment.[18] A student's previous academic performance, when observable, may capture many of these "unobservable" characteristics. This is why NCES commissioner Robert Lerner noted that NAEP score comparisons would not be valid without accounting for prior test scores that would adjust for unobserved student ability and discipline.

Another way to offset, if not overcome, the problem of being unable to randomize or control for all the relevant student characteristics is to compare the performance of students who have been both in charter schools and in regular public schools. If the pattern of student gains changes when students move from regular public to charter schools, or vice-versa, this could indicate the relative effectiveness of these school types.

As we describe below, studies at the state level have been conducted that utilize such methodologies, and they shed light on charter school effectiveness. Before turning to these, however, we review the findings of NCES itself when it performed its own analysis of the charter school NAEP sample.

The NCES analysis of the charter school NAEP sample

Do charter schools, in fact, attract students from racial or ethnic groups who are likely to be more or less advantaged socioeconomically than students of the same race or ethnicity in regular public schools? The AFT report was not able to address this question in August 2004 because cross-tabulations of race (or ethnicity) and socioeconomic status (i.e., eligibility for subsidized lunches) could not be performed with the data tool that NCES had made publicly available at that time. However, cross-tabulations are presented in the NAEP data that NCES released in December 2004 (NAEP 2005) and in unpublished data that NCES has made available to us. The data permit direct examination of the characteristics of charter and regular public school students to determine whether, as some prominent charter school advocates have claimed, charter schools attempt to educate the "disadvantaged of the disadvantaged" (Allen 2004c).

These examinations reveal that charter schools are more likely to be disadvantaged in that charter school students are more likely to be black: 31% of charter school students are black, compared to 17% of regular public school students (NAEP 2005, Table A-6).

Table 1 presents more detailed information than in the published NCES report on the distribution of students by income, race, and location in charter and regular public schools. It shows the share of students that are lunch-eligible for each race and ethnicity. The top row shows that charter and regular public schools, overall, have similar proportions of low-income students. Among students of all races there was a slightly larger share of charter school students (47%) who were lunch-eligible than of public school students (46%).

However, this similarity masks the fact that suburban and rural students in regular public schools are more likely to be low income than suburban and rural students in charter schools. In the central cities, the share of lunch-eligible children in charter and in regular public schools is identical — 65%.

Table 1. Percent of lunch-eligible students, by race and location

	Percent lunch-eligible		
	Charter schools	Regular public schools	Difference
Total	47	46	1
Central city	65	65	0
Urban fringe	29	36	-7
Rural	30	41	-11
All blacks	68	76	-8
Central city	72	83	-11
Urban fringe	49	64	-15
Rural	92	76	16
All whites	22	27	-4
Central city	39	37	3
Urban fringe	16	17	-1
Rural	18	27	-9
All Hispanics	72	77	-5
Central city	80	82	-2
Urban fringe	59	71	-12
Rural	22	76	-54

Note: Data are for students who took the NAEP 4th Grade Math Assessment and who reported whether they were eligible for free or reduced-price lunch.

Source: NAEP 2005; supplemented by unpublished data furnished to the authors by the National Center for Education Statistics.

As we noted earlier in this report, some charter school zealots have claimed that the reason that, in the AFT's August NAEP report, charter school test scores for black students were not higher than regular public school test scores for black students is that black students in charter schools were more disadvantaged than black children in public schools. But the newly available and more detailed NAEP data in Table 1 contradict this claim.

These data show that regular public schools have a greater share of low-income students than charter schools among each of the race and ethnic categories for which test scores have been reported: blacks, Hispanics, and whites. This suggests that any comparison of test scores, controlled only for race and ethnicity, between charter and regular public schools is biased in favor of, not against, charter schools, because charter schools have a *more advantaged* population among each racial group.

The composition of the black student populations is particularly important in this regard: while 76% of black students in regular public schools are low income, only 68% of black students in charter schools are low income. In central cities as well, black students are more likely to be low income in regular public schools (83%) than in charter schools (72%).[19]

For Hispanic students, Table 1 also shows that those in charter schools overall, and those in central city charter schools, are not more likely to be low income than those in corresponding categories of regular public schools.

We should be somewhat cautious about these conclusions in one respect. The data reported in Table 1 include only students who took the fourth-grade NAEP math exam and who reported whether they were or were not lunch-eligible. About 10% of charter school students and about 4% of regular public school students did not report whether they were eligible. We know of no plausible explanation for the difference in reporting rates between charter and regular public school students, and therefore have no basis for assigning non-reporters to the eligible or non-eligible category. When NCES (in NAEP 2005) and the AFT (in its August report) show different percentages than those in Table 1, they implicitly assume that all non-reporters are not eligible. It has been generally reported that the NCES analysis found that a slightly larger share of regular public school students (44%) were lunch-eligible than charter school students (42%). These percentages describe the number of students who were lunch-eligible as a share of the total of all students, including those who reported or did not report whether they were eligible. Table 1, however, to the extent it implies results for charter schools and regular public schools generally, implicitly assumes that students who do not report lunch eligibility have the same rate of eligibility as those who do report.

To test the extent to which this implicit assumption could be misleading, Appendix B includes two re-calculations of Table 1. One (Table B-1) shows the share of all students and all members of each subgroup (including non-reporters) who were lunch-eligible. (Data in this table correspond to the widely reported statistic from the NCES report that

42% of charter school students and 44% of regular school students were eligible.[20]) Despite the difference in reporting rates between students in charter schools and regular public schools, this appendix Table B-1 confirms the pattern established in Table 1 that charter school students are not more likely to be lunch-eligible than regular public school students.

A second table in the appendix (Table B-2) has re-calculated Table 1 using the most extreme "best case" scenario for charter school effectiveness. It assumes that *all* non-reporting students in charter schools were lunch-eligible, while *no* non-reporting students in regular public schools were eligible. While this assumption is implausible, Table B-2 shows that, even under such an extreme assumption, black students in charter schools are not more disadvantaged than black students in regular public schools. And in the central cities specifically, under such an extreme assumption, black students in charter schools are also not more disadvantaged than black students in regular public schools. Indeed, the opposite is the case.

To the extent that data are available, we can also conclude that, under this extreme assumption, Hispanic students in charter schools are no more disadvantaged than Hispanic students in regular public schools.

These results do not accord with the view of charter school proponents that charter schools enroll the "disadvantaged of the disadvantaged," unless this refers to low-income students in charter schools being more disadvantaged than the low-income students in other public schools. The NAEP data cannot address this possible claim.

Comparative studies of charter and regular public school demographics in individual states

Conclusions from national NAEP data regarding the demographic characteristics of charter school students have been confirmed and deepened in a variety of detailed state-level studies that have compared student performance in charter and traditional public schools. The demographic characteristics of students covered by these studies are summarized in **Table 2**. This table includes all state-level studies of charter school demographic characteristics that we were able to locate.

In general, to interpret this table, it will be helpful to keep in mind the following rule of thumb: if charter schools in a state have a larger share of minority students than do regular public schools in that state,

while charter and regular public schools have a similar share of socioeconomically disadvantaged students, then it is probable that the minority students in the charter schools will be less disadvantaged than minority students in regular public schools. This follows because minority
students are, overall, more likely to be disadvantaged than white students, so schools with a higher share of minority students would ordi-
narily be expected also to have a higher share of disadvantaged students.
If they do not have a higher share of disadvantaged students, then the
minority students in these schools are likely to be unusually advantaged.

Studies of charter schools in Massachusetts (Reville et al. 2004),
Illinois (Nelson and Miron 2002), and Pennsylvania (Miron, Nelson,
and Risley 2002) point out that there are considerable waiting lists to get
into many charter schools. This would facilitate selecting out potentially troubling students should charter schools wish to pursue such a
policy. Even if schools with waiting lists select students from the list by
lottery, if admission to the list is conditioned on advantageous student
characteristics (for example, a willingness of parents to participate in
school programs and a promise by parents to do so), schools can ensure
a population of students who are easier to educate than otherwise similar students who did not place their names on the list.

Table 2 shows the following for the 12 states studied and the District
of Colombia:

Arizona. Research on the total population of students in Arizona charter
schools (Solmon and Goldschmidt 2004) estimates that of students who
spent at least two of the three years 1999-2001 in charter schools, 40%
were minority (in Arizona, the vast majority of minority students are
Hispanic), compared to about 44% who were minority among students
who spent at least two of those years in regular public schools.[21]

California. Data developed by Tom Loveless (2003) and also independently by a team of RAND analysts (Zimmer et al. 2003), and including
all students in charter schools in that state, show that the proportion of
socially disadvantaged (as measured by students' lunch-eligibility and
parents' educational level) is essentially the same in charter and public
schools, although the percentage of black students in charter schools is
higher. These studies find that, among black students in California charter schools, a somewhat lower share are low-income than among black

Table 2. Findings on student characteristics in specific state studies comparing charter and regular public school performance

State	Higher percentage of black students in charter schools?	Higher percentage of Hispanic students in charter schools?	Higher percentage of socioeconomically disadvantaged students in charter schools?
Arizona		No [1]	N.A. [2]
California I	Yes	No	No
California II	Yes	No	N.A. [2]
California III	N.A. [1]	N.A. [1]	No
California IV	Yes	No	No
Colorado		No[1]	No
Connecticut	Yes	Yes	N.A. [2]
Dist. of Columbia I	N.A. [2]	No [5]	Yes
Florida	Yes	No	No
Illinois	Yes	No	No
Massachusetts	Yes	No	No
Michigan I	Yes [1]		No[3]
Michigan II	No [4]	Yes [4]	Marginally yes[4]
Michigan III	No[1]		No[3]
North Carolina	Yes	No	No
Pennsylvania	Yes[1]		No difference[6]
Texas I	Yes	No	N.A. [7]
Texas II	Yes	Marginally yes	Marginally yes
Wisconsin	Yes [8]	Yes	No [9]

Sources: Arizona: Solmon and Goldschmidt 2004; California I: Loveless 2003; California II: Zimmer et al. 2003; California III: Raymond 2003; California IV: Rogosa 2003, 2004; Colorado: Colorado Department of Education 2003; Connecticut: Miron and Horn 2002; District of Columbia I: Buckley, Schneider, and Shang 2004; Florida: Sass 2004; Illinois: Nelson and Miron 2002; Massachusetts: Reville et al. 2004; Michigan I: Eberts and Hollenbeck 2002; Michigan II: Bettinger 1999; Michigan III: Miron and Nelson 2002; North Carolina: Bifulco and Ladd 2004; Pennsylvania: Miron, Nelson, and Risley 2002; Texas I: Gronberg and Jansen 2001; Texas II: Hanushek, Kain, and Rivkin 2002; Wisconsin: Witte et al. 2004.

Notes:
[1] Arizona, California III, Colorado, Michigan I, Michigan III, and Pennsylvania show data only on the percentage "minority." We assume that this is largely a black minority in Michigan and Pennsylvania, and largely a Hispanic minority in Arizona and Colorado. We make no assumption about the preponderance of blacks or Hispanics in California; California III shows that the percent minority is lower in charter schools than in regular public schools
[2] Data on socioeconomic status in Arizona are represented by only two variables — "migrant" and "English not primary language" — in regression analysis but not presented separately. Likewise, data on socioeconomic status are not presented in the California II study, although they are used in the analysis. Data on socioeconomic background in Connecticut were collected from a sample of parents of charter school students but not compared with the background of students in comparable regular public schools. Data on black students in the District of Columbia were not collected because almost all students (84%) in the District are black.
[3] In Michigan I, no statewide socioeconomic status comparisons were provided. The lunch-eligibility comparison is between charter school students in a particular district and students in regular public schools in that district. Michigan III conclusions are consistent with those of

Table 2 (continued)

Michigan I; in Michigan III, the percent of lunch-eligible students is higher in charter schools than in regular public schools statewide, but lower in charter schools than in their host district regular public schools.
[4] Charter schools compared to public schools within five miles of the charter.
[5] Data on Hispanic students in the District of Columbia were not specifically collected; however, there is a lower proportion of Limited-English-Proficient (LEP) students in D.C. charter schools.
[6] Philadelphia charter schools have students with somewhat higher socioeconomic status than students in corresponding area regular public schools.
[7] Texas I reports a higher percentage of socioeconomically disadvantaged students in charter schools than in regular public schools, but the percentage for charter schools (Gronberg and Jansen 2001, Table 5) is only for those that report "a positive number of students economically disadvantaged (111 of 142 charter schools)," whereas the regular public schools figure is for all public schools. Thus, the figures are not comparable.
[8] Milwaukee charter schools have a lower proportion of black students; charter schools outside Milwaukee have a higher proportion of black students. Overall, charter schools have a higher percentage of black students.
[9] Both Milwaukee and non-Milwaukee charter schools have higher socioeconomic status when compared with corresponding area non-charter schools.

students in comparable public schools.

Raymond's (2003) analysis also does not support a claim that California charter school students are, on average, more disadvantaged than students in regular public schools. She shows that the percentage of minority students (black and Hispanic students combined) is lower in charter elementary schools than in regular public schools, but somewhat higher in charter middle schools. She also shows that the percent of lunch-eligible students is much higher in regular public elementary schools than in charter elementary schools, but somewhat lower in regular public middle schools than in charter middle schools.

Detailed estimates developed by Rogosa (2003, 2004) for the 2001-02 school year for all students in charter schools and in all schools (charter and regular public) who took the California state test are consistent with these other California analyses. (The data do not include students in chartered home schools who did not take state tests.) Rogosa finds that, as in other states, black students are over-represented in California's charter schools — 8% of students in all of the state's schools are black, but 16% of charter school students are black. White students are also over-represented in charter schools: 42% of charter school students are white, compared to 34% in all California schools. In charter high schools (ninth to 11th grades) the percentage of white students ranges from 39% to 47%, depending on the grade, whereas in all high schools they range from about 36% to 41% — the higher the grade in high school, the more whites. This pattern of more whites in charter schools is also true for primary and middle schools, where the percentage of whites increases in the upper grades. In all schools, the percentage of whites is 31% in second grade and steadily rises to 41% in 11th grade. In charter schools, the percentage of whites rises from 38% in second grade to 47% in 11th grade. Asian American and Latino students are under-represented in charter schools. Nevertheless, because Latinos are the largest group of students in California schools, there are almost as many Latino students in charter schools as white students.

Rogosa defined socioeconomic disadvantage either as eligibility for subsidized lunches or having no parent who completed high school. His data suggest that charter school students in California are less likely to be socioeconomically disadvantaged than students in regular public schools. This is the case for each racial and ethnic group (see **Table 3**). In elementary schools, the smallest difference is for black students and the largest for whites, the two over-represented groups in charter schools. Moreover, in middle schools, the proportion of disadvantaged black students in charter schools drops sharply compared to a much smaller decline in regular public schools.

From Rogosa's data, it cannot be argued that charter schools are taking in the most disadvantaged of the disadvantaged. About four-fifths of all California primary school students who are socioeconomically disadvantaged attend schools where half or more of the students are socioeconomically disadvantaged; the share among charter school students is less than three out of four.

The largest student ethnic groups — Latinos and whites — are less likely to be in charter schools with high socioeconomic disadvantage than they are to be in regular public schools with high socioeconomic disadvantage. So in the largest charter school state — California — there is no basis for claims that charter schools serve a more disadvantaged student population and that, as a result, charter school test scores should not be expected to be higher than regular school test scores.

Colorado. In this state, where the largest minority is Hispanic (22% of all students were Hispanic in 2000, compared to 6.5% of all students who were black), data on the total population of students in charter schools show that they enroll both a lower percentage of minority students and a

Table 3. Percent of students who were socioeconomically disadvantaged in California charter schools and all California schools, by race-ethnicity and by grade, 2002.

Grade	All	African Americans	Asians	Hispanics	Whites
California charter schools					
2-5	0.46	0.67	0.33	0.77	0.13
6-8	0.38	0.48	0.37	0.70	0.12
All California schools					
2-5	0.58	0.71	0.44	0.82	0.25
6-8	0.51	0.61	0.43	0.78	0.22

Source: Rogosa 2003, 2004. Charter school data are for all 341 charter schools in California in the 2001-02 school year. "Socioeconomically disadvantaged" is defined as having no parent who completed high school or being lunch-eligible, or both.

lower percentage of lunch-eligible students than do regular public schools (Colorado Department of Education 2003). Minority enrollment in charter schools has remained at 27% from the 1999 to the 2001 school year, whereas the minority percentage in regular public schools rose from 29% to 33% in that period (Colorado Department of Education 2000, 2001, 2002, 2003). The percentage of lunch-eligible students in charter schools is only 18%, compared to 28% in regular public schools; both figures have been fairly stable since the late 1990s. Furthermore, when charter schools are compared to regular public schools in the same school district, charter schools average a lower percentage of minority students in 27 of 39 districts and average a lower percentage of lunch-eligible students in 28 of 39 districts (authors' estimates from Colorado Department of Education 2003). The state Department of Education suggests that charter schools tend to under-report students who are lunch-eligible, but it is also possible that the minority students who do attend charter schools come from higher-income families than do those who remain in regular public schools.[22]

Connecticut. Miron and Horn (2002) drew a relatively large sample of Connecticut charter school students and a small sample of their parents in 1997-98 and again in 1999-2000. They found a much higher percentage of blacks and Hispanics in charter schools than in regular public schools statewide, mainly because of the location of the charter schools in high minority districts. They did not compare race, ethnicity, or parents' income and education to the demographic characteristics of comparable regular public schools.

District of Columbia. A detailed statistical comparison of all charter schools and regular public schools in Washington, D.C. (where as many as one-sixth of all students attend charter schools) deals directly with whether charter school students are more difficult to educate (Buckley, Schneider, and Shang 2004). This study finds no significant observable difference in educability between students in the two types of schools. On average, charter schools in the District of Columbia have a slightly higher percentage of lunch-eligible students, but slightly fewer special education and English language learners. (The study does not discuss these differences by race because almost all — 84% — of the District's students are black.)

Florida. In a large sample of schools and students (including all those in charter schools), the proportion of blacks is somewhat higher in charter schools, the Hispanic proportion is about the same, and the proportion of lunch-eligible students is lower in charter schools (Sass 2004).

Illinois. Nelson and Miron (2002) show that in Illinois in 2001-02 charter schools were located in communities that were larger and poorer and had more minority families. This was true both of the 15 charter schools that had been established in Chicago (enrolling 89% of the state's charter school students) as well as of charter schools established in other communities statewide (a charter school was established in each of seven other districts). A higher percentage of black students but a lower percentage of Hispanic students enrolled in charter schools than in regular public schools of the host districts. Charter schools also tended to have lower lunch eligibility than did regular public schools in the host districts. Furthermore, there was greater racial concentration in charter schools than in regular public schools in the host districts. This occurred primarily because of a higher concentration of black students in charter schools.

Massachusetts. Data from Reville et al. (2004) that include all charter school students in the state show that the actual percentage of black students in charter schools is higher, and the percentage of whites and Hispanics is lower, than would be expected if the proportion of charter school students from these groups were the same as the proportion in the school districts from which the charter schools draw their students. This is particularly true in Boston and other urban areas. Suburban Massachusetts charter schools have an over-representation of whites and an under-representation of minorities. However, Massachusetts charter schools serve fewer low-income students than their feeder districts. A smaller proportion of students in Massachusetts charter schools located both in urban and suburban areas come from low-income families than do students attending public schools in the feeder school districts. Since charter schools in Boston have an enrollment that is two-thirds black, compared to Boston regular public schools where 47% of students are black, and the proportion of low-income students is almost 10% lower in Boston's charter schools than in Boston's regular public schools, it follows that the black students attending charter schools in Boston probably come from somewhat higher-income families than do the black students in regular public schools.

Michigan. In a study of all 33 charter elementary schools and 19 charter middle schools that were operating in the school year 1996-97 (Bettinger 1999), the average proportion of lunch-eligible students in the charter schools was 57%, compared to 52% in public schools within five miles of the charter schools.

In a more recent Michigan study, researchers compared charter schools with regular public schools in the same district, not within five miles. They found that, although charter schools tend to be concentrated in the lower-income, minority districts, "the free lunch eligibility percentage and the nonwhite building enrollment percentage are quite comparable to the traditional schools in the districts where the charter schools are located," suggesting that within districts, students attending charter schools and regular public schools are not very different (Eberts and Hollenbeck 2002, 10).[23] The limited data from this study, however, do not permit a test of charter school zealots' claims that lunch-eligible black students in charter schools are more disadvantaged than lunch-eligible black students in regular public schools.

Findings in another Michigan study (Miron and Nelson 2002) are consistent with those of Eberts and Hollenbeck: the proportion of lunch-eligible students in Michigan is about the same for charter schools and for corresponding regular public schools (52% in charter schools, 53% in host districts).

North Carolina. An analysis of all third-grade cohorts tested over a five-year period shows that, despite the higher fraction of minority students in a typical charter school, the average education of parents of students in charter schools is considerably higher than that of students in regular public schools. In particular, black students attending regular public schools are likely to come from less-educated families than black students in charter schools (Bifulco and Ladd 2004).

Pennsylvania. Using data for all charter and regular public schools in the state, Miron, Nelson, and Risley (2002) compare the demographic characteristics of charter schools with the demographic characteristics of their host districts. About 50% of the charter schools in the state in 2000-01 were in Philadelphia, where most of the students attending charter schools are African American. Although Philadelphia was not analyzed separately from the rest of the state in this study, we used data reported therein to approximate an (unweighted for enrollment) average lunch eligibility in Philadelphia charter schools. For the 38 (of 39) charter schools in Philadelphia that reported lunch eligibility, the average eligibility is 68%, compared with 73% in Philadelphia's regular public schools. It appears, then, that students attending charter schools in Philadelphia are less likely to be lunch-eligible than students in Philadelphia's regular public schools.

Texas. Two studies based on total student populations in charter and regular public schools (Gronberg and Jansen 2001; Hanushek, Kain, and Rivkin 2002) show that charter schools have a higher percentage of black students than regular public schools, but Hispanics are slightly less likely to attend a charter school than a regular public school. In the 1999 school year, the percent of blacks in charter schools was 39% compared with 14% in public schools; the corresponding figures for Hispanics was 38% in charter schools and 40% in regular public schools (Gronberg and Jansen, 2001). The percentage of blacks in charter schools increased somewhat in the 2000 school year (Hanushek, Kain, and Rivkin 2002). Both studies also show a somewhat higher percentage of low-income students attending charter than regular public schools, although the Gronberg and Jansen results (59% socially disadvantaged in charter schools vs. 49% in regular public schools) are biased: their estimate compares the percentage of lunch-eligible students in all regular public schools with the percentage in only those charter schools that report serving disadvantaged students, excluding from their calculations over 20% of charter schools that serve no disadvantaged students.

Wisconsin. A recent study of all students in the state's charter schools in 2001-02 compared students' ethnicity and socioeconomic background at the school level (Witte et al. 2004). Outside Milwaukee, charter schools have a higher percentage of black students than do regular public schools (9% vs. 4%), a somewhat higher percentage of Hispanic students (6% vs. 4%), and a lower percentage of white students (78% vs. 88%). Yet the average proportion of lunch-eligible students is somewhat lower in charter schools than in regular public schools (18% vs. 20%). If students who are eligible for lunch subsidies are less likely to participate in charter than in regular public schools outside Milwaukee, then, although charter schools enroll more minority students, the minority students they enroll are probably less disadvantaged than minority students on average in these communities.

In Milwaukee itself, black students are less likely to attend charter schools and white and Hispanic students more likely. Black students in Milwaukee who attend charter schools are likely to come from more educated families than do black students in regular public schools. Like Boston, but in contrast to Philadelphia and the District of Columbia, the percentage of lunch-eligible students in Milwaukee is lower in charter schools than in regular public schools (46% vs. 72%).

Summary of demographic data from state-level studies

In sum, data from individual state studies do not suggest, on the whole, that the AFT or NCES-reported NAEP results understate charter performance for minority students because they are more disadvantaged. At least for the states for which data have been analyzed, charter school students from racial or ethnic minority groups are probably at least as advantaged as regular public students from the same racial or ethnic groups and, in many cases, probably more so. Because the 13 states (including the District of Columbia) described in Table 2 cover about 75% of the nation's charter school students, and because the state studies each generally covers the universe of charter school students in their states, the results are comprehensive.

That charter school students seem to be more advantaged than regular public school students is not in itself a reason to be critical of charter schools. A legitimate mission of charter schools could be to provide superior educational services to more advantaged students. But this is not the mission that many prominent charter school supporters claim; indeed, they argue the opposite. And while having more advantaged students should not, in itself, be thought a flaw in charter schools, this characteristic should predict higher charter school performance than that of regular public schools. That such a prediction is apparently not fulfilled is the issue with which we are here concerned.

In California, Connecticut, the District of Columbia, Florida, Illinois, Massachusetts, North Carolina, Pennsylvania, Texas, and Wisconsin, charter schools tend to cater more to black students and less to whites. But the average socioeconomic background of students in charter schools, as measured by parents' education or the proportion of lunch-eligible students, is, with some exceptions (the District of Columbia, one of the Michigan studies [II], and one of the Texas studies [II]), not significantly worse, on average, than the socioeconomic background of all regular public school students. Using the rule of thumb we set forth at the beginning of this chapter, we can conclude that charter schools tend to enroll the more advantaged of the disadvantaged.

If charter schools in the rest of the country were demographically like those in California, Colorado, Florida, Illinois, Massachusetts, Michigan (I and III), North Carolina, and Wisconsin, and if charter and regular public schools were equally effective, we would expect the NAEP scores for minority fourth-graders to be somewhat higher in charter schools than in regular public schools. But the NAEP scores in both types of schools are about the same for minority students. This could have one of two possible explanations. One is that minority students in charter schools might have unobserved characteristics that contribute to lower academic proficiency than minority students of similar socioeconomic status in regular public schools, in which case charter schools might not be performing below their predicted results for minority students. A second is that, if no such confounding variables exist, charter schools do in fact perform below their predicted results for minority students.

Are charter demographics over-stated because of a failure to offer the lunch program?

The data suggest one of two possibilities. The one suggested by NAEP data and by data from individual state studies is that, although the percentage of minority (especially black) students attending charter schools is higher than the percentage attending public schools, the average socioeconomic background of those students is *not* less advantaged than that of the minority students in regular public schools.

A second possibility is that there are measurement issues that lead to an understatement of the degree to which charter schools enroll low-income students. For instance, charter schools may not enlist otherwise eligible students for lunch subsidies to the same extent as public schools do (Eberts and Hollenbeck 2002; Colorado Department of Education 2000), or they are less accurate in reporting the rates of their student lunch eligibility (Colorado Department of Education 2003) or do not have free and reduced-price lunch programs. If that is true, disadvantage measured by lunch eligibility is biased downward in charter schools — students may seem to be non-poor when, in fact, they are eligible for lunch subsidies but are not receiving them, or their participation is not reported. If this is the case, there may be significant socioeconomic differences in favor of public schools, even for the same racial and ethnic groups, and it would help to explain why charter school academic performance was no better than regular public school performance, even after either race, ethnicity, or economic status (as measured by eligibility for lunch subsidies) had apparently been controlled.

We do not think that measurement errors are generating our conclusion that minority charter school students are probably more advantaged than their peers in public schools. There is no evidence of which we are aware establishing that charter schools deny lunch subsidies to children who should receive them. It is possible that charter schools that have only a small percentage of low-income children would find it too cumbersome to offer a lunch program, but this could not explain our finding, for example, that black students in central city charter schools are less likely to be lunch-eligible than black students in comparable central city regular public schools. Roy (2005), for example, finds that charter schools that reported no lunch-eligible students were likely to be located in communities that had above-average incomes, as judged by the lunch eligibility of their matched regular public schools. And one consideration leads us to think it plausible that charter schools would be more likely, not less so, to enroll eligible children in the lunch program: because parental participation is often a condition of charter school admission, parents can more easily be required to complete eligibility forms that may be ignored or overlooked by some parents of regular public school students.

Other evidence of the relative advantage or disadvantage of charter school students

Other evidence that charter schools tend to serve the least disadvantaged of students from disadvantaged populations comes from a study of locational decisions made by charter schools in the District of Columbia (Henig and MacDonald 2002). It finds that charter school operators are more likely to locate new schools in black and Hispanic than in white neighborhoods, but also more likely to locate new schools in neighborhoods that had relatively high rates of home ownership and families whose incomes were moderate, not extremely low. The authors offer no evidence that District of Columbia charter schools actually enroll children from their immediate neighborhoods but argue that, especially for poor families, there is a cost — transportation being primary — to attending schools that are not close by, so it is plausible to assume that there will be a higher proportion of children enrolling in a charter school who live reasonably close to it. Henig and MacDonald cite other research finding that, while all families tend to make convenience of location a primary consideration in choice of charter schools, for minority and low-income families it is a substantially greater consideration. Taking the location of charter schools into account, therefore, it is unlikely that charter schools in the District of Columbia are serving black students who are more disadvantaged than black students generally. If anything, the opposite is likely to be the case.

Another attempt to estimate the relative disadvantage of students in charter schools was based on comparing students' pre-charter school test scores to scores of comparable students in regular public schools. If students whose scores before they entered charter schools were lower than those of comparable students, it can be inferred that, on average, the charter school students were more disadvantaged than comparable students in regular public schools.

A recent study of Arizona's charter schools claims to make this comparison, and shows that students had lower test scores before they entered charter schools than did comparable students in regular public schools: "charter students generally started off with lower achievement than their traditional public school counterparts" and so higher charter school scores were all the more remarkable (Solmon and Goldschmidt 2004, 1).

However, the study drew its conclusions about charter school students' prior abilities from test scores of these students at the end of their first year in charter schools, not before they entered. These were compared to scores of students in regular public schools, also measured at the end of the year they spent in regular public schools. This is not an adequate way to measure student disadvantage. If charter school students made lower gains and regular public school students made larger gains during that year, it would appear that the charter school students began the year with more educational disadvantage than they in fact did.

The test score differences *at the end* of that initial year were adjusted for race, grade, immigrant status, and other variables. But the lower scores still may reflect a harmful effect of spending a year in a recently formed charter school rather than the prior academic disadvantage of a charter school student, controlling for socioeconomic and ethnic differences. The students who attend Arizona charter schools may be more disadvantaged academically, but we should be careful about basing that conclusion on their scores after they have already been in a charter school for nearly a full academic year. Several studies (Hanushek, Kain, and Rivkin 2002; Loveless 2003; Bifulco and Ladd 2004) have suggested that in the first year or two after a charter school is formed, students are not particularly successful.

Further, as Nelson and Hollenbeck (2001, 8) point out, commenting on similar Arizona data:

> Lower test score levels are clearly not sufficient evidence to conclude an absence of positive selection. Even though test score levels are lower for charter school students than traditional public school students, the former may still systematically differ from the latter in

unobserved ways. The fact that students and parents have chosen to attend charter schools suggests that the parents are interventionists: they have taken the initiative to transfer their students in the belief that they will get a better education. If such parent initiative is positively related to test scores, then the coefficient on charter schools will be biased upward. [24]

The North Carolina study (Bifulco and Ladd 2004) collected data on students who switched from regular public schools to charter schools. The results suggest that the effect of initially switching to a charter school from a regular public school does have a significant and large negative effect on student test performance. If we assume that this negative effect in North Carolina is also found in Arizona, it could explain much of the significant test score difference for public and charter school students at the end of the first year in Arizona. The North Carolina analysis suggests that a significant part of the "initial" differences in Arizona between charter and public school students may be a first-year charter effect, not the student's prior academic performance. The Arizona claims cannot be relied upon to support the idea that charter school students are more disadvantaged than public school students from the same broad demographic groups.

In a comparison of charter schools with regular public schools that are geographically closest and have similar racial compositions, Roy (2005) finds that, on average, charter schools have, in comparison to their matched regular public schools:

- higher proportions of black students (34% vs. 28%);

- higher proportions of white students (43% vs. 36%);

- lower proportions of Hispanic students (18% vs. 30%);

- lower proportions of lunch-eligible students (49% vs. 64%).

With specific reference to charter schools in central cities, Roy finds that these charter schools also have fewer minority students overall (more black but fewer Hispanic students) and fewer lunch-eligible students than their matched regular public schools.[25]

While charter schools as a whole may not enroll students who are more disadvantaged than demographically comparable public school students, there are certainly some, perhaps many, charter schools that enroll or attempt to enroll the more disadvantaged. One study found that, in Washington, D.C., small non-profit charter schools disproportionately served the most needy students, but for-profit charter schools and chains of schools (those that had expanded, or hoped to expand, to multiple locations) disproportionately served the less needy (Lacireno-Paquet et al. 2002). Perhaps the insistence of charter school zealots that the NAEP results obscured charter schools' enrollment of more disadvantaged children can be attributed to these advocates' reliance on valid, but unrepresentative, anecdotal accounts of exceptional charter schools.

The KIPP case

One network of schools — KIPP[26] — has been promoted by some charter school supporters as having students who are more disadvantaged than students in comparable regular public schools, yet whose test scores after being in KIPP are typically higher than scores for black and Hispanic urban children generally (Thernstrom and Thernstrom 2003; Fuller 2001; Education Trust 2003). This, they add, illustrates the remarkable results that a charter school can produce for typically disadvantaged children.

This view has been widely accepted. A *USA Today* (2005) editorial called KIPP Schools "probably the most successful charter schools in the U.S.," and claims that the KIPP instructional strategy "pays off. Three of every four KIPP graduates go on to college, compared with fewer than half the students in the neighborhood schools they left." If students at KIPP were truly representative of students in the neighborhood schools they left, these statistics would certainly suggest the superiority of such charter schools.[27]

To test our hypothesis that the disadvantage of charter school students is often exaggerated by zealous charter school advocates, we undertook an examination of these claims by the KIPP Schools and their admirers. (In undertaking and reporting on this investigation, it is not our intent to comment in any fashion on whether KIPP Schools are or are not more effective than regular public schools serving similar students. We find that, in important ways, KIPP students are not representative of students in regular public schools in disadvantaged communities, but this finding does not challenge claims that KIPP is effective.

Investigation of such claims is far beyond the scope of this report.)

Most KIPP Schools are middle schools that start with the fifth grade, and some, though not all, publish data showing the entering test scores of their students — fourth-grade scores in the students' previous regular public schools. An examination of these data reveals no pattern that would support an assertion that these schools systematically enroll children who are as academically challenged as students from similar race, ethnic, or income (i.e., lunch eligibility) backgrounds, and it certainly does not support a belief that schools like KIPP enroll the "disadvantaged of the disadvantaged."

KIPP Schools often publish "pre-KIPP" scores to show the gains students make on tests taken while enrolled in KIPP in the fifth, sixth, seventh, and eighth grades. It might be supposed that these "pre-KIPP" scores could then be compared to test scores of fourth-graders in neighboring schools to see if KIPP students were more or less disadvantaged than those from the same demographic groups in neighboring schools. Such a comparison is not always possible, however, because, in most cases when KIPP Schools publish "pre-KIPP" scores, the data are not based on end-of-year fourth-grade scores but on tests that KIPP itself administers to fifth-graders after the fifth-grade school year has begun.

It is impossible to know the extent to which KIPP's beginning-of-fifth-grade scores are comparable to end-of-fourth-grade scores at neighboring schools. It is plausible that the scores of disadvantaged students, like those enrolling in KIPP, at the beginning of the fifth grade would be *lower* than those same students' scores at the end of fourth grade, because disadvantaged children's scores often decline during the summer when learning from the previous year is not being reinforced and supplemented (Entwisle and Alexander 1992; Allington and McGill-Franzen 2003). The National Center for Education Statistics, in a recent summary of the literature on this topic, states: "A number of studies suggest that achievement gaps grow when children are away from school" (NCES 2004b).

If this "summer setback" characterizes KIPP students, then a comparison of beginning-of-fifth grade scores for KIPP students to end-of-fourth grade scores for regular public school students could make KIPP students seem more disadvantaged, relative to regular public school students, than they are in fact.

However, KIPP requires entering fifth-graders to attend a pre-KIPP three- to four-week program at the beginning of the summer prior to their enrollment in KIPP. The program is designed to get KIPP students accustomed to the KIPP discipline and routine, but it has some academic content as well. We cannot know whether the effect of this summer program offsets the achievement loss typically experienced by disadvantaged children. Because the summer program is brief and takes place at the beginning of the summer, cases where test scores of entering KIPP fifth-graders are lower than fourth-grade scores of students in regular public schools still may be attributable to summer setback, so the conclusion cannot be drawn from this that KIPP students are initially lower performing than comparable regular public school students. Similarly, if test scores of entering KIPP fifth-graders are slightly higher than fourth-grade scores of students in regular public schools, this may be attributable to the KIPP summer program, so the conclusion cannot be drawn from this that KIPP students are initially higher performing than comparable regular public school students. However, if differences between test scores of entering KIPP fifth-graders and those of fourth-graders in neighboring schools are large (either much higher or lower), it is unlikely that these differences are attributable solely to summer setback or to the brief KIPP summer program.[28]

This measurement difficulty can only be overcome for a few KIPP schools from which comparable data (end-of-fourth grade scores prior to enrolling in KIPP) are available. In those we were able to examine, entering fifth-graders had fourth-grade scores that were significantly higher than those of regular public school students with similar demographic characteristics.

For example, KIPP reports that, at its school in Baltimore, entering fifth-graders in 2002-03 had pre-KIPP (fourth-grade) median national percentile ranks of 42 in reading and 48 in math (Hahnel 2005). KIPP did not disaggregate these scores by socioeconomic status, but the school is 100% black. The Baltimore City school system reports that, in the spring of 2002, its black fourth-graders had a median national percentile rank of 36 in reading and 34 in math (BCPS 2002, Tables 22 and 28). Thus, entering students in the Baltimore KIPP school were more proficient in reading and math than typical black fourth-graders in Baltimore. In this respect, students at KIPP-Baltimore are not typical of Baltimore's black students overall.

One of the more widely heralded KIPP Schools is located in the

Bronx, New York, and headed by David Levin, one of KIPP's national founders. In *No Excuses*, Abigail and Stephen Thernstrom (2003) suggest that this school provides a model of how charter schools can excel beyond regular public schools in the same community. It "is in one of the city's worst high poverty neighborhoods," but shows that "it is possible to have public schools that are spectacularly good — at least if they are charter schools." Citing data provided by KIPP, the Thernstroms report that 66% of KIPP students were above grade level in math and 55% in reading by New York State standards, compared to 9% in math and 16% in reading for the district in which KIPP is located.

To understand whether this itself suggests superior performance, it is necessary to know whether KIPP students were unusually high performing before they entered KIPP-Bronx. In this case, as in Baltimore, it is possible to compare the fourth-grade scores of entering KIPP students to the fourth-grade scores of neighboring schools that are demographically similar. Such a comparison shows that KIPP students, as a group, enter KIPP with substantially higher achievement than the typical achievement of schools from which they came.

Table 4, column (j), compares the 2002 fourth-grade reading achievement of entering KIPP-Bronx students with the average reading achievement of fourth-graders in the 31 geographically closest elementary schools.[29] In only one of these 31 schools (Franz Sigel Elementary School) did a greater percentage of fourth-graders pass the New York State reading test than did entering KIPP students. On average, KIPP students seem to have substantially higher achievement before they enter KIPP than their peers in the schools they left behind. While 42% of entering KIPP students passed the fourth-grade reading test, only 28% of fourth-graders from these 31 neighborhood schools passed.

KIPP-Bronx attracts a higher percentage of black students (and a lower percentage of Hispanic students) than do other schools in its vicinity (see columns [d] and [e]). However, there are nine neighborhood schools where over 40% of the students are black. The proportion of fourth-graders who passed the state reading test is much higher for entering KIPP students (42%) than for students in these more racially comparable schools (25%).

Column [c] indicates four elementary schools (Melrose, Banneker, Quism, and Dunbar) that David Levin, the KIPP superintendent, identified to us as schools that send more students to KIPP than do other schools.

In each case, students who entered KIPP were more likely to have passed the New York State fourth-grade reading test than typical students in those schools. On average, only 31% of fourth-graders in these source schools passed, compared to 42% of entering KIPP students.

In some cases, parents enroll their children in KIPP after their regular public school fourth-grade teachers or principals recommend that they do so, because of KIPP's reputation for academic success. KIPP leaders claim that these teachers or principals are likely to recommend their least successful students, partly because of KIPP's reputation for being able to save such children from a failure to which they were otherwise headed. David Levin also speculates that, because neighborhood elementary schools include the fifth grade, teachers and principals are likely to recommend their more disruptive and academically unsuccessful students to KIPP as a way of ridding their schools of troublesome students before they entered fifth grade (Levin 2004a). By reducing the number of low-scoring students in these schools, such a practice would also help these regular public schools improve fifth-grade test scores for which they are being held accountable. Susan Schaeffler, executive director and founder of the Washington, D.C. KIPP school, says that principals of regular public schools in the District recommend that parents send their children to KIPP in cases where the children "aren't doing well in public schools" (Schaeffler 2004). "We have kids who are homeless, some who suffer from drug abuse [in their homes]. We're dealing with an inner-city population, the same kids the regular public schools have" (Rothman 2004b). Sarah Hayes, the school's principal, adds that, because KIPP has a reputation of succeeding with the most difficult children, parole officers refer children to KIPP (Hayes 2004). If these observations are consistently accurate, then KIPP students would be more disadvantaged than seemingly similar students from their demographic groups. At the very least, they would be no more advantaged.

We attempted to check these claims by interviewing teachers who were teaching or had taught at neighborhood regular public schools from which KIPP drew a relatively large number of its students. These interviews, with teachers from the Bronx, Washington, D.C., and Houston (where KIPP was first established) attempted to determine if students whom these teachers had recommended to KIPP, or whom these teachers knew had transferred to KIPP, seemed to be more or less able than typical students in their classes.[30] None of those we interviewed con-

Table 4. KIPP-Bronx Academy, compared with neighboring elementary schools (2002)

(a) Elementary school	(b) Distance from KIPP (miles)	(c) Initial KIPP source schools	(d) Percent black	(e) Percent Hispanic	(f) Percent free lunch	(g) Percent free and reduced lunch	(h) Percent female	(i) Percent Limited English Proficient	(j) Percent passing N.Y. State 4th-grade reading
KIPP-Bronx	0.0		53	47	74	94	58	0	42
KIPP source schools			37	61	91	96	49	17	31
Area schools with high black enrollment			46	53	90	98	49	16	25
All area schools			34	64	87	93	49	18	28
William Lloyd Garrison	0.0		30	67	86	87	53	11	33
Melrose School	0.3	yes	28	70	88	95	50	15	25
Franz Siegel	0.4		38	59	84	95	48	19	46
John Peter Zenger	0.5		35	64	87	93	50	11	22
Courtlandt	0.6		30	70	92	95	51	23	15
Benjamin Banneker	0.6	yes	38	60	87	93	47	14	29
George Meany	0.8		36	61	79	96	48	20	30
Basheer Quisim	1.0	yes	41	58	95	100	49	17	30
Eagle	1.0		37	61	91	98	51	16	20
Children's Literacy Center	1.1		18	81	85	81	46	20	14
Abram Stevens Hewitt	1.1		21	78	92	98	48	11	28
Edward "Pop" Collins	1.1		48	51	90	95	50	9	21
Juan Ponce De Leon	1.2		27	72	*	66	46	21	28
Jonathan D. Hyatt	1.2		39	60	80	90	45	13	40
Port Morris	1.3		26	73	85	95	52	18	41

School									
Mott Haven Village	1.3		27	72	75	89	45	14	32
CES 73	1.3		27	71	*	98	48	23	33
Bilingual School	1.4		10	89	87	92	51	39	16
Inocensio Casanova	1.4		21	78	78	77	49	17	28
Dr. Marjorie H. Dunbar	1.5	yes	37	62	*	95	51	21	38
Wilton	1.5		16	83	88	93	50	22	21
Jonas Bronck	1.6		43	56	94	89	49	10	24
Garrett A. Morgan	1.6		49	50	*	100	48	15	30
Morrisania	1.7		47	53	73	91	48	17	23
High Bridge	1.7		29	69	100	93	46	21	27
Charles James Fox	1.8		21	78	83	85	49	22	23
Claremont Community	1.9		46	52	91	100	44	16	22
Benjamin Franklin	1.9		47	53	96	99	51	22	22
George F. Bristow	1.9		47	52	83	100	52	19	24
Shakespeare	1.9		35	64	89	91	50	26	27
Theodore Schoenfeld	2.0		49	49	*	99	48	11	25

Sources:
b: Mapquest.com (because of one-way streets, some walking distances may be shorter).
c: Levin 2004a.
d, e, g, i: Data are school-wide, 2001-02 (NYSED 2004; NYCPS 2004).
f: Data are school-wide, 2001-02 (NCES 2004c; NYCPS 2004).
h: Data are school-wide (NCES 2004c; NYCPS 2004). Data are 2002-03 because they were the only data available for all schools considered.
j: KIPP a; NYCPS 2004.

Notes : Figures shown in column (i) for average passing rates of source, high-black, and area schools were calculated using fourth-grade enrollment weights (NYCPS 2004; not shown). Figures shown in columns (g and h) for percent female and percent Limited English Proficient (LEP) of feeder, high-black, and area schools were calculated using the total schoolwide enrollment weights (NYCPS 2004, not shown).

* For these schools, reliable data on free lunch participation are not available. NCES (2004c) reports very low percentages of free lunch eligibility for these schools, and NCES's report of combined free and reduced lunch eligibility is more than 20 percentage points lower than the NYCPS report of combined free and reduced lunch eligibility.

firmed David Levin's and Susan Schaeffler's claims that schools were systematically referring their more troublesome or lower-performing students to KIPP, or that teachers were motivated to urge such students to enter KIPP so that regular public schools would be rid of more difficult children.

On the contrary, teachers told us either that they referred students who were more able than their peers, or that the most motivated and educationally sophisticated parents were those likely to take the initiative to pull children out of the public school and enroll in KIPP at the end of fourth grade. A clear pattern to emerge from these interviews was that almost always it was students with unusually supportive parents or intact families who were referred to KIPP and completed the enrollment process. One fourth-grade teacher in a regular public school in the Bronx (one that Mr. Levin had identified as sending many students to KIPP) mistakenly believed that KIPP was designed as a "gifted" program suitable only for high-performing students. He said he had referred students to KIPP who needed more challenge than his regular school could provide, because these students were progressing faster than their peers. The teacher did not want his name used in this report because referring students to KIPP is frowned upon in his school; KIPP, he said, gets the "cream of the crop," and regular public schools are "losing most of the cream because KIPP is getting the top notch students" (Teacher1 2004).[31] This, of course, makes the regular neighborhood school's job more difficult in the fifth grade and beyond. Another teacher at a Bronx KIPP source school said that she personally declined to refer students to KIPP because doing so "brings the scores down" of the regular school — the students most likely to switch to KIPP are the more able students (Teacher2 2004). A teacher at a different Bronx school from which KIPP drew acknowledged that "I know that being bright is not a requirement, but…" she nonetheless used this a criterion for referral to KIPP and added that "parental involvement is the main ingredient and that is what they [KIPP leaders] want. It is the crucial factor in their success" (Teacher3 2004).

A former New York City teacher who referred several children to KIPP, summarized the emphasis she placed on selecting only students with more involved parents before she made such referrals (Teacher4 2004):

I learned that a kid who is really resilient with all the obstacles they face in their home life is important. I also thought about parents on the phone — do they have conversations with me? Are they involved? Do they come to back-to-school night? Do they get papers signed and turned back in? It was the academics and parent involvement.

We interviewed a former teacher at a Washington, D.C. elementary School, one of those identified by Ms. Schaeffler as a regular school from which a significant number of KIPP-D.C. students came. The teacher described 20 children whose parents she had urged to apply to KIPP. Of these, 15 applied and 13 were accepted. The teacher taught fourth grade and was also her school's student government advisor; all of the children she referred to KIPP were either in her class or members of the school student government. Not all were relatively high-achieving students, and many were children she believed were achieving below their potential. A few had serious health or social problems that made it difficult for them to fit in at their regular school, and the teacher felt that KIPP would make a special effort to help such children succeed. The teacher recalled that many of her referrals came from two-parent homes, a characteristic which was not typical of her students. Further, she noted that "[p]arental support is extremely important. This is the common denominator that all of the students I nominated have." When one student she referred to KIPP did not have such strong family support, the student got low grades in KIPP and returned to the regular public school after one year. On one occasion when KIPP had an opening midyear, Ms. Schaeffler telephoned the teacher to discuss a possible transferring student's ability to transition to a new school midyear, the emphasis being on whether the child had the unusually strong parental support needed for success (Teacher5 2004).

Teachers in Houston, site of the original KIPP school, echoed these themes. One who taught in a school serving disadvantaged children in Houston and who referred students to KIPP said that all the students she referred were above average (for their peers) academically. But still, she said, this was not the main consideration in her referrals (Teacher6 2004):

I think less about the kid and more about the parent. If parents aren't the type to be sure the kid would get there to the school on time and on Saturday and in the summer, I wouldn't refer them. The parents would have to be sure the kid was up on time to make the bus and be willing to get the kid to school on Saturdays and be sure to have a quiet space to get homework done.

A regular Houston public school teacher with whom we spoke thought highly of KIPP (he later left his regular public school and took a job teaching at a KIPP school) and wanted as many of his low-performing students to transfer to KIPP as possible, because he felt they would do better there than at his regular public school. In one year, this teacher reports (Teacher7 2004) that he contacted 100 parents to urge them to apply to KIPP:

> What is bothersome is that I wanted the low kids to go who were in need. When I talked to parents, the kids I thought most needed it, parents said stuff like "sounds too serious and he needs another year to grow up." Another student I had who we signed up, then at the last minute, the parent said it was too hard to get her to the bus stop to get her to the school. This was ridiculous, though, because the bus stops at [the regular public school where I taught] so it isn't hard to get her there. Those were two of the lowest-ability kids and they both signed up but then decided not to go. A lot of the kids who aren't doing so well, the parents didn't want to sign them up and send them. So the kids I got to go to KIPP were really good kids with high test scores and really good behavior. I felt bad because I didn't want to be skimming the best kids. My principal didn't want good kids to leave to go to magnet schools or other programs because then the school lost good test scores. A lot of the families were undocumented and some were illiterate. These are the parents who were not going to have the resources and contacts to be sure their child got what he needed, but I couldn't get very many of these parents to apply....Who ended up going to KIPP were kids with better-than-average test scores and parents who cared, motivated parents.

A puzzling aspect of Table 4 (see column [h]) is that KIPP-Bronx had a substantially higher proportion of female students (58%) in the fourth grade in 2002 than did neighboring schools, schools from which many KIPP students came, or nearby schools with a relatively high share of black students. Each of these groupings of regular public schools had

Table 5. Percent girls in KIPP schools (2002-03)

School	Percent girls
NYC-Bronx	58
Houston-KIPP	56
D.C.	56
Gaston, N.C.	53
Houston-3D	51
Newark	59
Baltimore	49
Denver	51
Austin	58
Helena, Ark.	61

Source: NCES 2004c.

Note: Data were not available for schools in Memphis, Oklahoma City, or Asheville, N.C.

student bodies that were 48% female. **Table 5** shows the percentage of female students in the 10 KIPP schools that had been established by 2002-03 (and for which data were available), and suggests that this may be a pattern throughout the KIPP school network.

A possible explanation was given by one of the referring teachers whom we interviewed. Boys whom the teacher had referred were apparently more reluctant to follow the teacher's advice and apply to KIPP than parents of girls who had been referred, because the parents tended to believe that their boys could get by on their own without being removed from the negative influences of neighborhood peers. Parents of girls, this teacher speculated, were more likely to believe that their children were in need of protection by being removed from the bad influences of the immediate neighborhood (Teacher5 2004).

The Houston school teacher, cited above, commented on this pattern after he moved to become a KIPP teacher:

[M]ost of our African American kids are not from nearby and they tend to be more middle class parents and mainly girls....I have heard theories that parents want to protect the girls more [by getting them out of the neighborhood]. I also think retention is a problem here in Houston, and it is usually the boys who are retained and if boys get too old, it is harder to get them to come [to KIPP]. I was saddened but I have a harder time with the guys. Maybe the girls are more mature. I wish we had more boys and more Spanish-speaking-at-home kids. For me it is always a struggle — for the middle class kids who come, the spot isn't really for them but you can't blame them for finding something better if their school is not the greatest.

Whether these teacher interpretations of the gender imbalance at KIPP are correct, the fact that enrollment is more heavily female is another factor that makes KIPP Schools unrepresentative of the neighborhood schools from which they draw. Typically, by eighth grade, girls in urban school systems have higher test scores (especially in reading) than boys. On the special NAEP assessment of urban students, fourth-grade girls and boys had nearly identical math scores (with boys having a tiny advantage), and the gender gap was not significantly different for the eighth grade. But girls had higher reading scores in the fourth grade, and this gap was even wider in the eighth grade.[33] (These scores are displayed in **Table 6**). If KIPP enrolls a disproportionate number of girls, its widely reported average test score gains throughout the middle school years, greater than those of regular schools, may partially be attributable to its gender composition.[34]

There is no evidence that KIPP officials consciously recruit a more advantaged student body, except to the extent that they require parental commitment that may be greater than that of typical parents in comparable regular public schools. KIPP often makes great efforts to recruit typical children, provided KIPP can be assured that parents will sign and abide by the KIPP contract. In Washington, D.C., KIPP faculty have stood outside neighborhood markets to attempt to recruit such children (Mathews 2002). In the early years of KIPP-Bronx, the school's faculty went door-to-door in the neighborhood to attempt to interest randomly identified and typical neighborhood families in the school. But as the reputation of KIPP-Bronx grew, this effort at representativeness was frustrated. Parents applied who were not typical, but who wanted their children to benefit from KIPP's unusual academic press. Under charter laws, KIPP was required to select randomly from those who applied; it could not turn away highly motivated children in order to save spaces for those recruited door-to-door (Levin 2004a).[35]

This discussion is not meant as a criticism of KIPP Schools. We do

Table 6. Scores by gender for selected cities, NAEP Trial Urban Assessment, 2003

I. Percent above basic:	4th-grade math			8th-grade math			4th-grade reading			8th-grade reading		
	Girls	Boys	Gender gap, girls vs. boys	Girls	Boys	Gender gap, girls vs. boys	Girls	Boys	Gender gap, girls vs. boys	Girls	Boys	Gender gap, girls vs. boys
Houston	69	70	-1	50	54	-4	50	46	4	61	49	12
New York City	65	69	-4	54	54	0	60	46	14	68	55	13
Washington, D.C.	37	36	1	29	29	0	36	26	10	55	38	17
Average (unweighted) of 3 cities	57	58	-1	44	46	-1	49	39	9	61	47	14

II. Percent above proficient:	4th-grade math			8th-grade math			4th-grade reading			8th-grade reading		
	Girls	Boys	Gender gap, girls vs. boys	Girls	Boys	Gender gap, girls vs. boys	Girls	Boys	Gender gap, girls vs. boys	Girls	Boys	Gender gap, girls vs. boys
Houston	17	19	-2	10	14	-4	19	17	2	17	11	6
New York City	19	23	-4	20	20	0	26	17	9	26	16	10
Washington, D.C.	7	8	-1	5	7	-2	13	8	5	13	8	5
Average (unweighted) of 3 cities	14	17	-2	12	14	-2	19	14	5	19	12	7

Source: NAEP 2004a; NAEP 2004b.

not suggest that its apparent effectiveness is solely attributable to its more favorable parental involvement, prior student achievement, or gender imbalance. KIPP supporters claim, and we have no evidence that disputes this, that KIPP provides children with the motivation and opportunity to excel that they might not have in their regular public schools. Our evidence is also not inconsistent with the notion that regular public schools might have a great deal to learn from KIPP's philosophy and strategy.[36] How to balance the opportunities for more talented children in schools of choice with the harm done to less talented children, remaining in regular schools, when they can no longer benefit from the influence of higher performing peers, is a difficult public policy issue in public education today. If KIPP-Bronx (and other KIPP schools) truly do attract the more talented or advantaged fourth-graders in their communities, KIPP resolves this policy dilemma no differently than New York City itself does by operating schools like Stuyvesant High School and the Bronx High School of Science that admit only students with high test scores. Nor is the KIPP solution different from that of New York City and many other urban school districts that create magnet schools to attract children with more motivation and parental support than typical children in disadvantaged communities. These magnet schools serve the more motivated children well, while leaving zoned public schools with a more difficult job because their enrollment concentrates disadvantage even more intensively.

Nor does the foregoing discussion of KIPP suggest that KIPP may not do an exceptional job of educating urban black fifth- to eighth-graders once they transfer from their regular public schools. Students may well make more progress in KIPP than they would have made if they remained in their regular public schools. However, the assumption, made by some charter school supporters, does not hold up to scrutiny that this must be the case if KIPP test scores are high because KIPP students enter the school with lower achievement than demographically comparable students in public schools.

Certainly, there may be some KIPP schools where students do enter with lower achievement than that of typical students in the schools from which they came. It is possible that, were we able to obtain data from other KIPP schools, or for other years, or if we were able to contact a wider group of teachers who referred students to KIPP, evidence would have emerged that in some cases KIPP students are more disadvantaged than comparable students from neighboring schools. The only claim we make here is that this is apparently not systematically the case, and it may not be the case in most instances.

If the apparent KIPP pattern is typical of charter schools generally that serve minority and low-income children, then a failure of charter schools to post high average NAEP scores cannot be explained away by a claim that charter schools serve children who were more disadvantaged, in unobservable ways, than demographically comparable students in regular public schools. Rather, it is more likely that, if KIPP is in fact unusually effective, its higher-than-predicted test scores are offset in charter school averages by other charter schools that are ineffective.

In sum, there is no consistent anecdotal or systematic evidence to support the claim that, on average, charter schools recruit students who are more challenged academically than those in traditional public schools serving the same student pool. Parents moving their children from public to charter schools could be more likely to do so if their children are doing poorly, but even in these cases the more motivated, demanding, and somewhat better educated parents are those more likely to notice poor performance. Interpreting "initial" lower test scores of students in charter schools as indicating that charter school students are especially disadvantaged is also risky, particularly if "initial" is not carefully defined to mean only "prior to entering" a charter school, because the first year in a new school may have a significant negative effect on students' performance.

CHAPTER 5

What we know about relative charter and regular public school student achievement

The NCES's own analysis of charter school NAEP scores

On December 15, 2004, the National Center for Education Statistics released its own report on charter schools, using the NAEP results from the 2003 pilot study (NAEP 2005). Despite NCES Commissioner Lerner's earlier critique of the AFT report, and his promises to overcome its flaws by providing simultaneous controls for race and economic status and by controlling for prior test scores, the NCES report provides neither. Using analytic tools apparently no more sophisticated than those used by the AFT, but correcting some data in the NCES database,[37] the new NCES report affirms the findings of the earlier AFT report in its essential details. As in the AFT study, when the sample is broken down into racial and ethnic groups, the differences in scores for each group attending charter and regular public schools are, in most cases, not statistically significantly different. As in the AFT study, lunch-eligible students who attend charter schools score significantly lower than lunch-eligible students who attend regular public schools. As in the AFT study, students attending central city charter schools scored significantly lower in math than students in central city regular public schools and lower, but not significantly so, in reading.

Indeed, the only major difference in the results of the two studies was that the overall reading score difference between charter and regular public schools is estimated as 7 points higher for public schools in the AFT study (and statistically significant), whereas it is 5 points higher in the NCES study (and not statistically significant). In the NCES study, when special education students were not included, the difference in reading scores, with charter school students lower, was statistically significant.

Using the published data as well as unpublished NAEP data made available to us by NCES, **Table 7** presents test score comparisons between charter and other public school students in greater detail than is available in the published NCES report. For each racial or ethnic group the scores are presented for students eligible or not eligible for lunch subsidies, and, for each of these income categories, the scores are provided by location. So, for instance, the table compares the charter and regular public school scores of students who are low-income whites and reside in urban fringe communities, who are low-income Hispanics who reside in central cities, and so on.[38]

Charter school zealots, as discussed above, have tried to explain away the fact that charter school scores are no better than or lower than those of regular public schools by invoking a student composition argument — charter schools tend to serve disadvantaged minority, low-income, mainly central city students. We have shown above that this composition argument is not valid. What Table 7 shows is that charter school students have the same or lower scores than other public school students in nearly every demographic category. Only one difference between charter and regular public school students is statistically significant, and in this case (black charter school vs. black regular public school students who are not lunch-eligible in central cities) the scores of charter school students are lower. So, even if the composition of students were the same in charter and other public schools, the overall scores would be no better for charter school students and in some cases would be even lower (though mostly not enough to be statistically significant).[39]

Of particular importance is the fact that the scores of low-income black students are lower in charter schools in both math and reading; low-income black students in central cities also score lower in both math and reading, although the differences are not statistically significant. The same can be said for Hispanic and white students. Students in nearly every category score lower in charter than in regular public schools, except for low-income whites in the urban fringe and non-poor Hispanics in reading (but not in math). Again, these differences are not statistically significant. But it is noteworthy that the pattern of results are that charter school scores are lower, and it can be said, with reasonable confidence, that students in charter schools do no better than similar catego-

Table 7. Test scores of students in charter and other public schools by race, eligibility for free or reduced lunch, and location, 2003

	Mathematics			Reading		
	Charters	Other public	Difference (charters less others)	Charters	Other public	Difference (charters less others)
White						
Eligible	230	231	-1	209	213	-3
Central city	225	231	-6	201	211	-11
Urban fringe	234	231	3	218	213	4
Rural	n/a	n/a	n/a	n/a	n/a	n/a
Not eligible	245	247	-2	231	232	-1
Central city	241	248	-6	231	232	-2
Urban fringe	247	249	-2	232	234	-2
Rural	240	245	-5	230	230	1
Info N.A.	243	245	-2	226	230	-4
Black						
Eligible	210	212	-2	188	193	-5
Central city	208	211	-3	188	191	-3
Urban fringe	218	214	4	n/a	n/a	n/a
Rural	n/a	n/a	n/a	n/a	n/a	n/a
Not eligible	220	227	-6	208	211	-3
Central city	217	225	-8*	208	207	0
Urban fringe	226	229	-3	205	214	-9
Rural	n/a	n/a	n/a	n/a	n/a	n/a
Info N.A.	219	219	0	198	199	-1
Hispanic						
Eligible	216	219	-3	194	196	-2
Central city	216	218	-2	195	196	-1
Urban fringe	215	219	-4	190	195	-5
Rural	n/a	n/a	n/a	n/a	n/a	n/a
Not eligible	229	232	-3	215	213	3
Central city	227	231	-4	215	208	7
Urban fringe	229	232	-3	n/a	n/a	n/a
Rural	n/a	n/a	n/a	n/a	n/a	n/a
Info N.A.	n/a	n/a	n/a	n/a	n/a	n/a

* statistically significant at the 5% level.

Source: NAEP 2005, and unpublished data provided to authors by the National Center for Education Statistics.

ries of students in regular public schools.

The new NCES data also fail to confirm claims that the performance of charter schools improves as these schools accumulate experience: in both math and reading, charter schools that have been providing instruction for four years or more report lower scores than new charter schools. This would seem to indicate that charter schools do not perform better as they gain experience and/or that newer charter schools have a smaller proportion of disadvantaged students.

Evidence from state-level studies regarding the achievement of charter school students

On the policy views of researchers

In the previous section of this chapter, we reviewed how the NAEP data, whether reported by the AFT or by NCES, seem to show that charter schools do not improve achievement overall. Yet despite the flaws, appropriately noted by zealous charter school advocates, inherent in drawing conclusions about school quality from point-in-time test scores that are poorly adjusted for student characteristics, it seems that the conclusion, suggested by NAEP, that charter schools perform more poorly on average than regular public schools is consistent with several state-level comparative studies of charter and regular public school academic achievement. Some of these state-level studies are not limited to making point-in-time comparisons of score levels in particular grades and have used standardized test scores that also permit some inferences about annual gains.

We discuss these studies here, including several that were carried out by supporters of charter schools and by researchers employed by or affiliated with policy institutes or advocacy organizations that promote charter schools.[40] This is inevitable: researchers tend to study phenomena in which they are interested. We do not claim, as the Charter School Leadership Council claimed about the AFT NAEP study, that this research therefore involves a "conflict of interest" (CSLC 2004). We agree, as the Charter School Leadership Council urges with respect to the AFT study, that such research should be subjected to "a credible independent review" before publication, but note that few, if any, of the studies on which we report, including those that purport to confirm the superiority of charter schools and that were cited by the Charter School Leadership Council as refuting the AFT results, were subject to such review.[41]

The Center for Education Reform's *New York Times* advertisement (see Exhibit A on p. 11), criticizing coverage of the AFT's report on charter school NAEP scores, stated that "[t]o date, we lack definitive evidence on the effectiveness of charter schools, in part because they are so new and so varied." But a similar statement could be made about regular public schools — that we lack definitive evidence about them in part because they are so varied and are experimenting with so many new programs. Yet conclusions about the effectiveness (or lack of it) of regular public schools are rarely withheld for that reason.

Description of state-level studies of charter school achievement

The assertion in the *New York Times* advertisement about the lack of evidence on charter schools was also curious because signers of the advertisement, specifically Eric Hanushek, Caroline Hoxby, Thomas Loveless, Margaret Raymond, Jonah Rockoff, and Simon Slovacek, had themselves previously developed and published considerable evidence on charter school effectiveness. In addition, Caroline Hoxby was about to publish a study of charter school achievement at the time of the advertisement's publication. We describe these studies below and summarize them and others in **Table 8**. Most of the evidence presented there, when examined carefully, shows that even charter schools that have been established for three to four years — long enough, according to the zealous charter school advocates, to have worked out the kinks and be accountable for academic results — at best achieve test scores that, on average, are no better than those achieved by regular public schools attended by students with similar racial, ethnic, and economic backgrounds.[42]

In the following discussion of Table 8, we describe each study's estimates of comparative point-in-time achievement levels in charter and regular public schools, and of comparative achievement gains in charter and regular public schools. The methodologies used by these studies differ not only because of different choices made by the authors but also because the available data in each state differ. As we discussed above, the greatest impediment to comparisons of achievement or achievement gains between the treatment group (charter school students) and the con-

Table 8. Relative student performance in charter and regular public schools (RPS), by state, late 1990s-early 2000s (Part 1 of 4)

State	Average scores in charter schools compared to RPS	Test score gains in charter schools compared to RPS	Controls for selection bias and other factors	Effect of age of charter school
Arizona	Negative (analysis limited to reading).	Positive (highest for those who start out in charter, switch to RPS); highest growth difference in early grades.	Controls for ethnicity, migrant, language, grade, special ed, gifted, student absenteeism.	No estimate.
California I	Positive for conversion charter schools; negative for start-up charter schools in each of three years, 1999-2000, 2000-01, and 2001-02.	Gains of scores adjusted for race and socioeconomic status are lower in charter schools in 1999-2000 to 2001-02, but not significantly so.	School means adjusted for race, ethnicity, and socioeconomic status.	No estimate.
California II	Conversion charter schools positive in elementary reading, negative in math. Start-up charter schools similar in reading, significantly negative in math.	Negative but not significant for either type of charter over the three years, 1999-2000 to 2001-02. Negative charter effect on gains of longitudinally matched students except for secondary reading.	Controls for race/ethnicity, socioeconomic and gender differences among students. Longitudinal student gain scores for several large school districts, controlling for student fixed effects.	No significant effect.

California III	Charter schools perform about the same as same-district public schools in elementary and middle schools but lower in high schools.	No significant difference at the elementary and middle school level; charter school students had significantly larger gains in high school in 1999-2001.	Gains analysis limited to schools that had scores for three years. Controls for percent minority, socioeconomic differences, school size, and percent credentialed teachers.	No estimate, but analysis is limited to charter schools in existence for at least three years.
California IV	Conditioning on race and socioeconomic disadvantage, charter school students' academic performance is somewhat lower, statewide, for all ethnic groups in primary schools and the same or somewhat higher in middle schools.	Gains of students in charter primary schools in 1999-2002 is slightly higher than in regular public schools, but lower in charter middle and high schools than in regular public middle and high schools. The gains pattern by level of schooling holds when conditioning on student and school socioeconomic level.	Gains analysis is limited to schools that had scores for 1999, 2001, and 2002 (93 schools); conditioned on socioeconomic differences among students and for socioeconomic level of school; estimates by grade and level of schooling.	No estimate, but analysis is limited to charter schools in existence for at least four years.
California V	For students in schools with at least 50% of students who are lunch-eligible, charter schools score significantly lower.	Slightly higher score gain in 1999-2001 in charter schools with at least 50% of students who are lunch-eligible, compared to similar regular public schools.	Limited to comparing charter and regular public schools with at least 50% of students who are lunch-eligible.	No estimate.

Table 8. Relative student performance in charter and regular public schools (RPS), by state, late 1990s–early 2000s (Part 2 of 4)

State	Average scores in charter schools compared to RPS	Test score gains in charter schools compared to RPS	Controls for selection bias and other factors	Effect of age of charter school
Colorado	Students in charter schools somewhat outperform students in regular public schools in primary and middle school grades in reading, math, and writing on Colorado Assessment Test. But comparison has weak controls for student ethnicity and socioeconomic background.	No gain in charter school scores relative to regular public school scores from 1998-99 to 2001-02 in 4th-grade reading and writing and 7th-grade reading and writing. Increase from 51 to 86 charter schools.	Attempt to compare schools with similar percentages of minorities and lunch eligibility, but comparisons were hampered by small number of charter students in many categories. Many charter schools do not administer tests.	No estimate.
Connecticut	Results vary by grade and subject, but generally 4th-grade charter and host district regular public schools have similar scores. Charter schools do somewhat better in 6th-grade math, better in 8th-grade math, and not as well in 10th-grade subjects.	Trends in average test scores between 1997 and 2001 in 4th grade were not significantly different for charter and regular public schools. Charter schools have higher gains over three and four years in 6th-grade math, 8th-grade (all subjects), and 10th-grade writing, science, and math. Charter school gains are higher	Comparisons are between charter schools and host district regular public schools. No controls for race, ethnicity, or socioeconomic background of students in schools, except for the fact that all comparisons are between charter and regular public schools in the same district. Comparisons for 4th, 6th, and	Positive for most charter schools.

Connecticut (cont.)		when the 4th-grade score in 1997, 1998, and 1999 is compared to 6th-grade scores two years later but are mixed compared to gains in regular public schools in host districts from 6th to 8th grade over the same two year period.	8th grade are based on seven charter schools; 10th-grade comparisons are based on nine charter schools.	
District of Columbia II	A higher percent of students in charter schools than in regular public schools scored "below basic" (the lowest category) on SAT 9 in 2000, even when controlling for SES level in the school.	A higher percent of regular public schools than charter schools improved their scores from the fall of 1999 to the fall of 2000 in both reading and math.	No controls for socioeconomic status on improvement scores. No differentiation by student grade either in the comparison of 2004 scores or in the estimates of improvement in achievement.	No estimate.
Florida	N.A.	No significant difference in reading; somewhat negative for mathematics.	Controls for observed and unobserved student differences through fixed effects model. Controls for student mobility between schools.	Positive and significant.

Table 8. Relative student performance in charter and regular public schools (RPS), by state, late 1990s–early 2000s (Part 3 of 4)

State	Average scores in charter schools compared to RPS	Test score gains in charter schools compared to RPS	Controls for selection bias and other factors	Effect of age of charter school
Illinois	On two tests in 1998-2000 (ISAT, PSAE), charter schools scored below or somewhat lower than comparable regular public schools; in Chicago, charter schools scored above regular public schools on ITBS in 2000-01.	Charter schools in existence in 1997 had test scores that declined somewhat relative to scores in comparison public schools from 1998-99 to 2000-01. Charter schools in existence in 1998 had test scores that increased relative to scores in comparison schools, but these charter schools still scored below comparison schools in 2000-01.	Controls for average school free and reduced-price lunch, percent white in schools, and percent LEP in schools.	No estimate.
Michigan I	Negative, 4th-grade, math and reading; 5th-grade, science and writing in every year, 1996-97 to 2000-01.	Negative for 5th-grade science and writing scores in 1999-2000, controlling for 4th-grade test a year earlier in math (paired with 5th grade science) and reading (paired with 5th-grade writing)	Student race, lunch-eligibility, gender, district fixed effects, school resources; no unobservable selection bias correction	Positive, but small.

Michigan II	Negative or neutral for 4th- and 7th-grade math and reading	Negative or neutral for 4th-grade reading and math and 7th-grade math and reading (1998); positive for 7th-grade reading, 1999. Charter schools show higher gains in 4th- and 7th-grade math for initially low-scoring students.	Student race, lunch-eligibility; pre-charter test in same school. No selection bias correction, but does use pre-charter test as control. Compared with public schools within five miles of charter.	No estimate.
Michigan III	Average four year (1995-96 to 1998-99) pass rate lower in charter schools in 4th- and 7th-grade math and reading and 5th- and 8th-grade science and writing	Slightly positive for 4th-grade math and slightly negative for 4th-grade reading and 7th-grade math and reading, somewhat negative for 5th-grade science and very negative for 5th-grade writing, same for 8th-grade science and writing.	Compared charter schools with schools in same district; no controls for student socioeconomic status or race.	Positive but small.
North Carolina	Significantly negative for both reading and math, controlling for ethnicity, gender, parent education, school mobility.	Negative for both reading and math, controlling for ethnicity, gender, parent education, school mobility, student fixed effects; negative for students observed entering a charter school; highly negative for students observed leaving a charter school.	Comparison of students who attended both a charter and regular public school, controlling for student race, ethnicity, gender, grade, parent education, student mobility, and student fixed effects. Students observed entering and leaving charter schools in a given year.	Positive.

Table 8. Relative student performance in charter and regular public schools (RPS), by state, late 1990s-early 2000s (Part 4 of 4)

State	Average scores in charter schools compared to RPS	Test score gains in charter schools compared to RPS	Controls for selection bias and other factors	Effect of age of charter school
Pennsylvania	Slightly negative scores for charter schools, compared with demographically and geographically similar public schools.	Charter schools' test score gains are slightly higher than in demographically and geographically similar public schools in the period from 1997-98 to 2001-02.	Comparisons with demographically and geographically similar public schools.	Positive for first two years of operation.
Texas I	In 1997-2000, reading and math scores are lower in charter schools, comparing across all charter schools and comparing at-risk students in charter schools with at-risk students in regular public schools.	Gains of movers from regular public schools to charter schools are negative; positive for movers from charter schools to regular public schools. Generally, gains for at-risk students staying either in regular public schools or charter schools from year to year are similar in both math and reading.	Comparison of at-risk students in charter and public schools. Estimate, with very small sample of charter students, student and school fixed effect models. These show that at-risk charter schools make larger gains than non-at-risk charter schools.	Positive.

Texas II	Negative math and reading for state charter schools; positive for district charter schools. Not statistically significant overall. Not adjusted for student differences.	Negative for state charter schools in reading and math; positive for district charter schools in math, insignificant in reading; no significant difference by ethnic group.	Student race/ethnicity, gender, grade, lunch-eligibility, student fixed effects, school mobility; accounts for students who attended both RPS and charter.	Positive and large; state charter schools younger on average— explains much of difference.
Wisconsin	Generally positive school average 4th-grade reading, language, math, science, and social studies; more mixed results for 8th-grade in same subjects.	No gain estimates.	School average race, ethnicity, lunch-eligibility. No selection bias correction.	No school age variable.

Sources: Arizona: Solmon and Goldschmidt 2004; California I: Loveless 2003; California II: Zimmer et al. 2003; California III: Raymond 2003; California IV: Rogosa 2003, 2004; California V: Slovacek, Kunnan, Kim 2002; Colorado: Colorado Department of Education 2000, 2001, 2002, 2003; Connecticut: Miron and Horn 2002; District of Columbia II: Henig et al. 2001; Florida: Sass 2004; Illinois: Nelson and Miron 2002; Michigan I: Eberts and Hollenbeck 2002; Michigan II: Bettinger 1999; Michigan III: Miron and Nelson 2002; North Carolina: Bifulco and Ladd 2004; Pennsylvania: Miron, Nelson, and Risley 2002; Texas I: Gronberg and Jansen 2001; Texas II: Hanushek, Kain, and Rivkin 2002 Wisconsin: Witte et al. 2004.[1]

[1] There are no achievement data on Massachusetts charter schools in this table, although we reported demographic data in Table 2. To the best of our knowledge, no study compares charter school achievement with regular public school achievement in Massachusetts.

trol group (regular public school students) is selection bias. The best studies are those that most closely compare students in the treatment and control groups who would be likely to do equally well academically were they to be in the same academic setting.

Unlike Miron and Nelson (2002), who attempt to rate the quality of such studies on a scale from 1 to 5, we merely describe the kind of controls and methods that the studies utilized and, in those cases where others have raised legitimate critiques of the methodologies, discuss those as well. Studies that use individual student data and are thus able to estimate gains in the same students' performance from grade to grade, to control for student fixed effects (thereby controlling for observed and unobserved student attributes that are invariate over time and might affect achievement gains), and are able to compare the same students passing from charter schools to regular public schools and vice-versa are most likely to eliminate selection bias. Some studies in Table 8 fulfill these conditions, but most do not. Even so, it is possible to have some confidence in comparisons of student achievement in charter and regular public schools if estimates of absolute achievement levels and achievement gains are made within the same racial, ethnic, and social class groupings for students in the two types of schools.

Studies in nine states — Arizona, California (II and IV), Colorado, Florida, Michigan (I), North Carolina, Pennsylvania, Texas, and Wisconsin — specifically estimate differences in performance of students in charter and regular public schools. Studies in California (II, III, and V), Connecticut, the District of Columbia, Illinois, Michigan (II and III), Pennsylvania, and Wisconsin compare results by school averages rather than on the basis of individual student scores.[43] Table 8 summarizes the results and how each study corrects for selection bias. State by state, the research shows the following:

Arizona. Student reading achievement in Arizona charter and regular public schools has been compared in grades 3 to 11 from 1997-98 to 1999-2000 (Solmon and Goldschmidt 2004). The analysis was limited to students for whom test scores were available in all three years. Students were divided into eight "attendance groups," including those who attended a charter school in all three years (4% of the sample), those who attended a regular public school in all three years (80% of the sample), and six groups of various combinations of attendance at charter and regular public schools during this period. Controlling for minority status, grade, migrant status, limited English proficiency, absenteeism, and several other variables, students in charter schools had considerably lower SAT-9 reading scores in the initial year (1997-98). The study also estimated gain scores over the three-year period for each student, controlling for the demographic and other variables mentioned above, and focused on the effect of the eight patterns of attendance in charter and regular public schools. It found that students who stayed in a charter school for the three years had significantly greater gains than students who stayed three years in a regular public school. However, students who spent either one or two years in a charter and then transferred to a regular public school made even bigger gains, suggesting that three years in a charter school is not necessarily the optimum educational pattern, even for making larger gains. Gains were estimated to be higher in the lower grades. Despite their greater gains, at the end of the three years charter school students still scored lower than regular public school students.[44]

California. Mathematics and reading scores in two types of state charter schools — conversion schools (regular public schools that converted to charter status) and start-up schools (schools that had not previously been regular public schools but had started up as charter schools) — were compared with student test scores in regular public schools (California I: Loveless 2003). In each year, 1999-2000, 2000-01, and 2001-02, using school means and controlling for race and socioeconomic background, start-ups had significantly lower scores than regular public schools and conversion schools had significantly higher scores.[45] (However, Loveless notes that conversion schools were often only permitted to convert if their scores were high in the first place. Conversion charter schools are established regular public schools that convert to charter status in order to be freed of some rules and regulations that apply to other schools.) Overall, charter schools scored lower than regular public schools, but not significantly so. There were also no significant differences in gains in scores made by either kind of charter school compared to regular public schools.

According to the RAND charter school study (California II), at the elementary level, conversion charter schools in California have higher reading performance but lower math performance than regular public schools (Zimmer et al. 2003). Students in start-up charter schools that are classroom-based perform as well in reading as students in regular public schools, but they perform worse in math. Students in charter schools that have part of their schooling outside the classroom (for example, charter schools designed to enroll children who are mostly schooled at home, or alternative high schools that serve youths at great risk of dropping out) do consistently worse in both reading and math tests than all classroom-based charter or regular public schools.

Unlike much charter school research, the RAND study meets important quality requirements specified in the *New York Times* advertisement by comparing students in charter schools with students in regular public schools over multiple years (1999-2002) and by controlling for students' race and ethnicity, parental education, and English-learner status, and whether the current year is the student's first at the school. The analysis also adjusts for overall trends in test scores from year to year. Unlike studies in other states, the RAND study finds only small differences in test scores for elementary grade charter schools that have been in existence longer. In addition, the RAND researchers estimated gains on California's Academic Performance Index for schools in each year (1999-2000, 2000-01, and 2001-02). They found that, in the first year, charter schools had larger gains than regular public schools, but these were not statistically significant; in the second two years, charter schools had smaller gains than regular public schools, but again these differences were not statistically significant (Zimmer et al. 2003, Appendix C).

In addition, the RAND study estimates test score gains for the same students in 1998-2002 in six California school districts (including two large districts, Los Angeles and San Diego) that provided student identifier codes. RAND researchers applied several models, including a student fixed-effects model and a random-growth model, to estimate the net effect of a student being in a charter school during all or part of this period. The researchers found no significant effect of charter schools on elementary reading scores, a positive charter school effect on reading in secondary schools, but large negative effects on math scores for both charter elementary and secondary schools.

Raymond (2003) uses gains in school averages by type of school in California (III). Unlike the Loveless (California I) or Zimmer et al. studies of California (II), she does not distinguish by type of charter (conversion or start-up) but does estimate the charter school effect on Academic

Performance Index (API) gains from 1998-99 to 2000-01 for all schools in the same school district. She includes all socioeconomic groups in her analysis. She also performs this comparison by level of schooling. Her results show lower gains (but not significantly so) in charter schools at the primary and middle school level, but much higher gains in charter schools at the high school level. Raymond also found that charter school students have lower gains in schools with higher percentages of lunch-eligible students.

Rogosa, however, has shown that Raymond's results were incorrectly estimated.[46]

Rogosa's own (2003, 2004) data on California charter and regular public school achievement for the 2001-02 school year (California IV) are consistent with the NAEP national estimates.

Table 9 provides greater detail from Rogosa's calculations than Table 8; it compares scores of charter and regular public school students on a composite of test scores in literacy, mathematics, science, and social studies, calculated from California's individual student test score database. To make these estimates, Rogosa calculated a quasi "academic performance index" (API) for each grade by using the same estimation rules as the state uses to calculate a school's official Academic Performance Index (the measure used in the state's accountability system), but considering each grade as a school. The calculations show that, on average, students in charter schools did somewhat less well on tests in 2002 than students of corresponding race, ethnic, and socioeconomic background in regular public schools. In grades 2-5, socioeconomically disadvantaged black and white students in charter schools had about the same composite scores as socioeconomically disadvantaged black students in regular public schools. Socioeconomically disadvantaged Asian-origin and Latino students in charter schools had composite scores that were about 4-5% lower than their counterparts in public primary schools.[47] The results are similar when we compare socioeconomically disadvantaged students who attend schools with high rates of socioeconomic disadvantage.[48]

Using these more accurate comparisons of student test scores than is possible with available NAEP data (Rogosa's data have better demographic controls than NAEP, but the analysis still suffers from having scores from only a single year), Rogosa finds that disadvantaged students in charter primary schools do somewhat less well than such stu-

Table 9. Ratio of estimated API-type test scores of students in California charter schools to scores of students in all California schools, by race-ethnicity, socioeconomic disadvantage, and grade, 2002.

Grade	All	African Americans	Asians	Hispanics	Whites
All charter schools/all California schools					
2-5	0.96	0.98	0.98	0.95	0.95
6-8	0.99	0.98	1.00	1.00	0.96
Socioeconomically disadvantaged students in charter schools / socioeconomically disadvantaged students in all California schools					
2-5	0.95	0.99	0.96	0.95	0.98
6-8	0.99	1.01	1.01	1.00	0.99
Socioeconomically disadvantaged students in charter schools with high socioeconomic disadvantage / socioeconomically disadvantaged students in all California schools with high socioeconomic disadvantage					
2-5	0.95	1.00	0.96	0.95	1.02
6-8	1.01	1.04	1.05	1.01	1.07

Source: Rogosa 2003, 2004. See notes for Table 3. Schools with high socioeconomic disadvantage are defined as schools in which at least 50% of students are socioeconomically disadvantaged. Data for the bottom panel come from 63 charter schools where at least 50% of students were socioeconomically disadvantaged for three consecutive years.

dents do in public primary schools, on average, and that this is especially true for Latinos, the largest socioeconomically disadvantaged group in California schools. This conclusion is consistent with the NAEP estimates.

In another California report (V), Slovacek, Kunnan, and Kim (2002) estimated that charter schools where at least 50% of students were lunch-eligible gained 67 points on the state's Academic Performance Index (API) in 1999-2001, from a level of 496 points to a level of 563 points. Corresponding regular public schools gained only 64 points, from 531 to 595. On this basis, Slovacek, Kunnan, and Kim (p. 3) concluded that:

> California charter schools are doing a better job of improving the academic performance (as measured by API) of California's most at-risk students, those who are low-income, than non-charter California public schools....Student achievement (as measured by API) in California's low-income charter schools is, on average, improving at a faster rate than in similar non-charter schools.

Rogosa, however, has demonstrated that methodological errors here, too, make the Slovacek, Kunnan, and Kim results unreliable.[49] Yet even if the latter's data were correct, a gain of an extra three points every two years (1.5 points a year) suggests that it would take another 20 years for charter schools in California to close the gap of 32 points in API between charter and regular public schools for this group of students. To argue that schools scoring so much lower than regular public schools are "doing a better job" would make sense only if Slovacek, Kunnan, and Kim could show that charter schools made greater gains than public schools for students whose initial scores were similar. It is possible, however, that regular public schools with similar demographic characteristics and similar initial test scores also made higher gains than regular public schools with somewhat higher initial test scores. Further, it is unclear that the three-point difference in gain is attributable to a charter school effect: because the comparison is between schools where lunch eligibility could range anywhere from 50% to 100%, even a small demographic change in charter or regular public schools during that two-year period could have produced this very small difference.

Colorado. Students attending charter schools in Colorado have generally performed better than students in regular public schools since the late 1990s, when the Colorado Department of Education began to make comparisons. In recent years, the department has compared charter and regular public schools with similar percentages of students who were minority or socioeconomically disadvantaged. More than half of Colorado's charter school students are in schools with the fewest number (the lowest quintile) of minority and lunch-eligible students, whereas less than one-third of Colorado's public school students attend such schools. In this group, charter school students performed about the same as regular public school students in most grades. In schools with greater percentages of minority and lunch-eligible students (higher quintiles), the results were mixed (Colorado Department of Education 2000, 2001, 2002, 2003). Because charter school students are less likely to be minority and lunch-eligible than regular public school students, even within quintiles, controlling for student race, ethnicity, and lunch-eligibility within these quintiles would probably show that students of similar family background do the same or better in regular public schools.

Connecticut. Miron and Horn (2002) were able to compare average scores in charter schools to scores in host school districts over a four-year period, 1997-98 to 2001-02. There were 12 charter schools in Connecticut in 2001-02. Of these, seven schools with fourth, sixth, and eighth grades and nine schools with a 10th grade had at least three years of data. Improvements in fourth-grade point-in-time scores from 1997 to 2001were similar for charter and comparable regular public schools, but improvements for sixth-grade math scores and for all subjects in eighth grade were greater for charter schools. Improvements in scores for 10th-grade charter school students were more mixed when compared to those for students in host district public schools. Comparative gains for school cohorts (for example, gains of 1999 sixth-graders compared to 1997 fourth-graders) were consistently higher for charter school sixth-graders in 1999, 2000, and 2001 when compared to fourth-graders two years earlier. The gains for charter school eighth-graders from their sixth-grade performance, when compared to similar gains in host districts' regular public schools, varied between cohorts. Nevertheless, none of the comparisons controlled for the socioeconomic composition of the schools.

District of Columbia. A study of the 30 charter schools that had been formed by 1999-2000 (Henig et al. 2001) shows that, across schools categorized by the socioeconomic level of their students, charter schools had a much higher proportion of students than regular D.C. public schools scoring in the lowest category (below basic) on the SAT 9 exam in the spring of 2000. The results are not reported by grade. The study also shows that a smaller proportion of charter schools than regular public schools improved their test scores in 1999-2000, although these improvements were not controlled for the socioeconomic backgrounds of students or for their grade levels. (However, more than 80% of students in regular public schools and more than 90% in charter schools were black in 1999-2000.)

Florida. Sass (2004) compared longitudinal test score gains for students in charter and regular public schools, controlling for their demographic characteristics and their mobility between schools. He estimated the increase in test score gains associated with attending a charter school, holding student characteristics and student mobility constant. Sass did not compare the specific situations of students who attended both charter and public schools, but controlled for those student characteristics that do not change over time. He found that being in a charter school in Florida has little effect on reading, but is somewhat negative in mathematics (Sass 2004).

Illinois. Nelson and Miron (2002) compared average test scores in charter schools to average scores in demographically comparable schools in host districts. Illinois had relatively few charter schools (22) from 1998-99 to 2000-01, and only 13 of them reported test scores. On two different tests used in Illinois, students in charter schools had about the same or lower levels of absolute achievement than students in comparable regular public schools in each of the years 1998-99, 1999-2000, and 2000-01. In terms of changes over time, charter schools that were in existence in 1997 lost ground relative to comparable regular public schools over the three years; charter schools that were in existence in 1998 made gains relative to comparable regular public schools in the same period. The Chicago Public School district administered the Iowa Test of Basic Skills in 2000-01. On that test, a higher proportion of Chicago charter school students scored at or above national norms in both math and reading than did the proportion of students in comparable regular public schools.

Michigan. Three studies using different methodologies found largely lower test score levels in charter elementary and middle schools than in comparable regular public schools. Two of the studies (Michigan I, Eberts and Hollenbeck 2002; Michigan II, Bettinger 1999) controlled for student race, ethnicity, and socioeconomic background, in addition to comparing charter schools with regular public schools in the same district (Michigan I) or with regular public schools within five miles of the charter school (Michigan II). Miron and Nelson (Michigan III , 2002) also compared charter school scores with those of public schools in the same district, but did not control for student socioeconomic status or race. Michigan I focused mainly on the charter school "effect" on student test scores in individual years (1996-97 to 2000-01) but also estimated individual fifth-graders' test scores in science and writing, controlling for the same students' test scores a year earlier in math (paired with science) and reading (paired with writing). It found that charter school students had lower gains than fifth-graders in district-matched regular public schools. Michigan II estimated gains across cohorts over two years. It found mixed results, including positive relative gains for initially low-scoring charter school students in fourth-grade science and math. Michigan III compared gains across cohorts in charter schools on several tests in several grades in the late 1990s. Except for fourth-grade math (slightly positive), students in charter schools made lower gains than students in regular public schools in the same district.

North Carolina. Bifulco and Ladd (2004) analyzed a large universe of students that included the third-grade cohorts for five years, 1996-2000, following them to the eighth grade or to the 2001-02 school year, whichever came first. Besides end-of-grade reading and math test scores, the data include the students' grade, gender, race or ethnicity, parents' education, whether the school was a charter or regular public school, and a school identifier. Thus, Bifulco and Ladd were able to track individual students over time and identify whether they were attending a charter or regular public school in any given year. They were able to compare gains that the same students made in charter and in regular public schools, because about 65% of students in the sample who spent some time in a charter school between 1996-2000 also spent at least a year in a regular public school during that period. To help correct for selection bias, they used repeated observations on individual students to control for individual fixed effects. The study found that across all students, grades, and years, students in charter schools scored significantly lower on both the reading test (0.16 standard deviations) and math test (0.26 standard deviations). They also found gains to be significantly lower in charter schools on both tests. The negative effect of being in a charter school was larger when the student fixed effects model was used. For the large number of students who changed from a regular public school to a charter school or vice-versa in a given year, Bifulco and Ladd estimated gains controlling for the fact that the change itself may have had a negative effect. The net effect of a charter school for those who had entered a charter school in the beginning of that year was significantly negative on both reading and math scores but less than 0.1 standard deviations (0.062 for reading and 0.097 for math). For those students who had left a charter school at the end of the year to enter a regular public school the following year, the negative effect on their test scores during the year they spent in the charter school was almost three times as large — about 0.16 and 0.27 standard deviations for reading and math scores, respectively.

Pennsylvania. Here, gains were slightly higher for geographically and demographically similar charter schools than for regular public schools. The differences are small and are observed in the first two years of a charter school's operation. Even with the slightly greater gains, charter school students average somewhat below comparable regular public school students in the same geographic area (Miron, Nelson, and Risley 2002).

Texas. In schools chartered by school districts, as opposed to those chartered directly by the state, students perform better than students in regular public schools. But when all charter schools in the state are considered, both those chartered by districts and those chartered by the state, there is no significant achievement advantage for charter schools (Hanushek, Kain, and Rivkin 2002). Gronberg and Jansen (2001), in an earlier analysis of charter schools in Texas, also found that, in general, gains in reading and math were similar for charter and regular public school students who stayed in either type of school for a three-year period.

Wisconsin. Results suggest that fourth-graders in charter schools are more likely to be proficient on state tests than those in regular public schools, and they do slightly better compared to regular public school students in the same school districts. The eighth-grade differences are more mixed, with regular public school students doing better in some subjects, especially in 2001-02 (Witte 2004).

In sum, except for reading scores (only) in California conversion schools (California II), sixth- and eighth-grade math scores in Connecticut charter schools, Colorado charter schools, district-chartered schools in Texas (Texas II), and fourth (but not eighth) grade in Wisconsin, the available state-level studies find primary-grade students in charter schools performing consistently below primary-grade students in regular public schools, even when scores are adjusted for differences in student demographics that tend to influence academic achievement. So the state-level studies generally support the conclusion suggested by the NAEP data that charter school achievement is no better than public school achievement.

In terms of the more rigorous criteria we invoked earlier, almost all the state-level studies also find that student *gain scores* are no higher or even lower in charter schools than in regular public schools.

Seventeen state studies were able to follow students (intra-cohort), grades (inter-cohort), or schools (inter-cohort) over time — Arizona, California (I, II, III, IV, and V), Connecticut, District of Columbia (II), Florida, Illinois, Michigan (I, II, and III), North Carolina, Pennsylvania, and Texas (I and II). Only seven of these (Arizona, California II, Florida, Michigan I, North Carolina, and Texas I and II), however, estimate test score gains for a single cohort of students as they progress from year-to-year — true "gain scores." Six of these studies estimate that gains were the same as or lower in charter schools than they were in regular public schools. The only exception was Arizona, where the estimates suggest that students in charter schools, especially in the lower grades, made larger gains than students in regular public schools. The other 10 studies (as well as California II) made inter-cohort estimates at either the grade or school level. Of these 11 studies, four showed larger gains for students in charter schools than in regular public schools: California (III), where only secondary-level charter schools made larger gains than regular public schools; California (V); Connecticut; and Pennsylvania. As noted earlier, however, the methodology and results in the two California studies (III and V) seem questionable (see notes 46 and 49 on pages 157-158).

In addition to these 17 studies, we were also able to estimate, from annual reports of the state department of education, gains for Colorado in the percentage of charter and regular public school students scoring at the proficiency level over a four-year period. These are inter-cohort comparisons (same grade each year) for fourth- and seventh-grade reading and writing achievement (no inter-cohort comparisons were made available for other tests). The results show charter school students with higher pass rates on the Colorado state test than regular public school students from 1998-99 to 2001-02, but the charter school advantage declined from the beginning to the end of this period.

In three of the studies with individual student longitudinal test score gain data — the two Texas studies and one from North Carolina — the authors also compared student performance gains for students who switched: students who attended both charter and regular public schools during the period covered by the data.[50] It is easily understandable that students in a "switch year" (when they move from a charter to a regular public school, or vice-versa) may not do as well as they might have otherwise, because switching schools is disruptive. The Texas I study, however, shows that students switching to charter schools did worse, whereas students switching to public schools did better. The North Carolina study shows that charter school students had significantly lower gains in reading and math, on average, than the gains students had made when enrolled in traditional public schools (whether they had switched from charter to regular public schools, from regular public to charter schools, or had remained the entire time in a charter or a regular public school). Of all students who attended both types of schools, however, those with the lowest gains were in the year spent in the charter school for those who switched from a charter to a regular public school.

This last finding illustrates why point-in-time score-level comparisons can be so misleading. Charter schools may find it easier to push out students who are not performing well, and this de-selection could depress public school score levels in the year after a student leaves a charter school. Regular public schools, however, must accept all children except in the most severe cases. In our interviews with teachers at regular public schools from which KIPP drew enrollment, for example, teachers noted that some KIPP students had returned or been returned to regular public schools for disciplinary or academic failure (Teacher2 2004; Teacher5 2004). There are no data that would permit us to compare charter and regular public school effectiveness by distinguishing voluntary switchers from those who are pushed out of charter schools and back into the regular public school system.

More surprising, those who switched from a regular public to a charter school also did worse than students who remained in regular schools. The academic cost of attending a charter school is lower the longer the charter has been in existence, but at least in North Carolina and in state charter schools in Texas (I), the influence of charter school availability on student academic achievement has been generally negative. Because students who switch are the same students in different circumstances, there is little selection bias except insofar as students who switch schools may be facing unusual conditions in other aspects of their lives that could negatively affect their academic performance.

Although not a state-level study (and thus not included in Table 8 or in the discussion of the studies described in it), Hoxby and Rockoff

(2004) analyzed student test score gains in 2000-02 in three Chicago charter schools enrolling a total of about 2,000 students in grades K-8 in two of the schools and K-12 in the third school. The innovation in this study was that Hoxby and Rockoff compared students in the charter schools with students who applied to these charter schools but who, because the applications exceeded the number of places, were not chosen in a lottery to determine admissions. Thus, the students in the charter schools were a random selection of a group of students who applied. Hoxby and Rockoff find that the charter school students made larger gains in math if they were admitted into second or third grade and in reading if they were admitted in kindergarten or first grade. Students admitted in other grades did no better or worse.

Age-of-school influences on charter school student achievement

As we noted above, if charter schools seem to be less effective than regular public schools for demographically similar students, a reasonable explanation could be that many charter schools are new and experiencing start-up pains. They require time to become stable before being held accountable for student achievement. Yet this consideration is less straightforward than it first appears. One way in which a charter school can benefit from its experience is by gaining insight into the type of student who would most benefit from (or who is least likely to be a problem for) the charter school's particular approach. Recruitment and counseling of prospective students can become more sophisticated as a school matures, making it more difficult to make comparisons of effectiveness with regular public schools whose students are demographically similar. Nonetheless, comparisons of mature charter schools with regular public schools can provide important information about charter school effectiveness that is obscured by comparisons that include all charter schools.

Seven studies of charter schools that include a variable for age-of-school (Florida, two studies from Michigan [I and III], North Carolina, Pennsylvania, and two from Texas [I and II]) show that the longer a charter school has operated, the smaller is the disadvantage in student performance compared to regular public schools.

California (II) analyzed mature elementary and secondary charter schools of two types: conversions from regular public schools and schools that had initially come into existence as charter schools (termed start-up charter schools). At the elementary level, only charter schools that had been converted from regular public schools for at least several years did slightly better than regular public schools. Older start-ups did worse at both the elementary and secondary level than regular public schools; older secondary conversion charter schools did worse as well.

On the whole, state-level evidence indicates that even when charter schools have been in existence for three years (the maturity cutoff suggested by some charter school supporters), their test scores are still at least no higher (in Florida, Michigan, Pennsylvania, and Texas) and, in North Carolina, lower, on average. In California, the results vary by type of school and level.

However, in the analysis of NAEP charter school data released by NCES in December 2004 (NAEP 2005), an opposite conclusion is reported: charter schools that have been instructing students longer report lower fourth-grade test scores than do new charter schools, although the report does not provide information needed to test for statistical significance. Because the NCES NAEP sample is more recent (2003) than data used in the state-level studies reporting higher scores for more established charter schools, a possible interpretation is that the demographic characteristics of charter schools are changing over time, and more recently established charter schools are more white and suburban than charter schools that have been in existence for longer. Or it may be that, in this respect, the states in which state-level studies of charter schools have been conducted are not representative of the national NAEP sample — although this is unlikely because state-level studies have been conducted in the large charter school states of Arizona, California, Colorado, Michigan, and the District of Columbia. Other possible interpretations are that the NAEP finding is not generalizable from the fourth grade to all school levels, or that, in fact, the NAEP results are correct that charter schools don't improve with age.

Nonetheless, there could be many individual charter schools with the potential for success whose test scores are initially low during a start-up period. But an argument that schools should be expected to have lower scores when they have start-up difficulties should also apply to many unstable regular public schools that serve transient student populations, for student mobility has an effect on performance that is similar to that of new leadership and faculty in start-up schools.

Exempting charter schools from accountability because of start-up pains might be valid, but only to the extent that student transiency resulted from charter schools being new, not to a tendency of charter schools to churn students more than do regular public schools. If the reason students are new to charter schools is not because the schools themselves are new but because even established charter schools tend to be revolving doors for students to a greater extent than are regular public schools, then zealous charter school advocates cannot use student transiency as an explanation of low achievement for which the schools should not be held responsible.

The authors of many state-level analyses we have reviewed point out that school switching is quite common; the most extreme case is Arizona, where one-fourth of all students changed schools during each of the two years under study, and half of all students changed schools once during the two years under study. In Texas and North Carolina, a high percentage of students also move in and out of charter schools and, as in Arizona, movement is significantly related to the achievement gains the student makes in a particular year. In Texas, however, the rate of movement in and out of charter schools is greater than in and out of regular public schools, the opposite of Arizona.

It might be expected that charter schools would reduce student mobility, because charter school students can remain in their schools even after their families have moved to different neighborhoods. In contrast, children who attend regular zoned public schools do not usually have the option of remaining in the same school. But this basis for stability, provided by charter schools, can be offset if choice becomes more of a habit for families who once exercise it. The data suggest that school shopping by charter school parents may be a more powerful influence than the opportunity to remain in a school of choice when residence changes, so on balance, charter schools increase student mobility.

Because changing schools generally has a significant negative impact on academic achievement, not only on the individual students who change schools but on other students in the schools, Bifulco and Ladd (2004) suggest that a downside of choice may be that, by increasing school mobility, any positive impact that comes from more school options (i.e., from the existence of charter schools) could be offset by the negative influence of increased school movement.

This problem is exacerbated by the relatively large number of charter schools that fail or that close for non-academic reasons. As we describe below, while only a small number of charter schools are closed by public authorities for academic shortcomings, a much larger number close because of financial or other mismanagement. At the beginning of the 2004 school year, for example, a chain of 60 charter schools in California suddenly went bankrupt, leaving 6,000 students scrambling for schools to attend. Student records were lost in the process (Dillon 2004). In another case, also in 2004, two successive charter school closures in a Los Angeles low-income black community left some 100 students having to find a new school twice in a period of three months (Hayasaki 2004). Such disruption will undoubtedly depress the achievement of these students as well as that of the students in the schools whose classes were unexpectedly reconstituted to accommodate their unplanned-for new classmates. Charter schools overall would have to post dramatically superior performance to offset the educational costs of closures like these. And further, in the case of the displaced students in these cases who were eventually placed in regular public schools, not in other charter schools, the educational costs of this charter school collapse will show up mostly in the lower average achievement of regular school students, not in lower average achievement of charter school students.

The competition effect

Some supporters of charter schools have suggested that, independent of how charter school scores compare to those in regular public schools, charter schools provide an overall benefit because, by competing with public schools, particularly in low-income districts, charter schools may stimulate regular public schools to improve. Caroline Hoxby (2001, 2003) argues that in Michigan and Arizona, in districts with relatively high percentages of charter school enrollment (6% or more), public schools made greater gains in test scores over several years after charter school competition occurred. If this were the case, then students in charter schools could be doing better than they would have done in regular public schools if no charter schools existed, but students who remained in regular public schools once charter schools were established could be doing better as well.

Sass' (2004) preliminary findings in Florida support the notion that the competition effect is positive and statistically significant. Attempting to correct for the possible endogeneity of charter school location (charter schools tending to locate near low-scoring public schools), he tests whether students in regular public schools with more charter enrollment in their vicinities make greater gains than students in regular public schools with less competition.

However, evidence presented in other state-level studies does not seem to support the existence of such a positive effect of competition from charter schools. The North Carolina study estimates the effect on public school student test scores over time as a function of the distance from the nearest charter school and of the number of charter schools within five miles. The estimates show no significant effect on public school student test score gains of having more charter schools within five miles of a public school, but the study also notes that the intensity of competition from charter schools is not great.

Evidence from two studies in Michigan, one of the states studied by Hoxby, also suggests that her results are anomalous. One of these (I) estimates the competition effect of the presence of a charter school in a district on fourth- and fifth-grade public school scores over a three-year period. It finds the effect to be negligible, with the exception of some small positive effects detected for fifth-grade scores only. This is a weak test of competition, but the study found no significant impact on public school scores of charter schools in the district.

A second Michigan study (II) estimates the effect of the number of charter schools within five miles of a regular public school on the public school's test score gains from October 1997 (termed the "pre-charter" score) to April 1998 and to April 1999, compared with 1996-97. In Michigan II, Bettinger uses an instrumental variable to correct for the possibility that charter schools locate near poorly performing regular public schools.[51] Again, the study finds no positive significant competition effect on public school performance.

If Hoxby is correct that the competition effect only kicks in when 6% of the students in a district attend charter schools, the North Carolina result may stem from not meeting this condition. However, there is also no reason to think that Hoxby's arbitrary 6% cut-off is the most appropriate one.[52]

It is also possible that Hoxby's finding is not confirmed in the Michigan studies because a competition effect pertains only to districts with at least 6% of students attending charter schools. But that may be an artifact of Hoxby's use in Michigan of district averages as the unit of analysis, rather than individual student performance (controlling for race, ethnicity, and socioeconomic status), as in the Michigan I and II studies. In Hoxby's study, 34 out of 597 Michigan districts had 6% or more charter school students. There may have been other unobserved variables acting to increase test scores in those districts in addition to the fact that they had a higher percentage of charter school students.

Segregation

Nelson and Miron (2002) found a greater racial concentration of black students in Illinois charter schools than in comparable regular public schools. The North Carolina and Texas studies note that students tend to attend charter schools that are more racially homogeneous than the regular public schools. "Thus, it appears that the charters in Texas have led to some additional racial and ethnic concentration, but it does so importantly because of increased black concentration in charters selected by black students" (Hanushek, Kain, and Rivkin, 2002, 15).

The North Carolina study estimates that "...the average black student who enrolls in a charter school in North Carolina moves from a traditional public school that is 53% black to a charter school that is 72% black, while the average white charter school student moves from a school that is 28% black to one that is 20% black, thereby exacerbating racial segregation" (Bifulco and Ladd 2004).

As noted above, Rogosa (2003, 2004) found that in California, socioeconomically disadvantaged students in charter schools were more likely to be in schools with less concentrated socioeconomic disadvantage than socioeconomically disadvantaged children in regular public schools. However, this characteristic — more socioeconomic integration in charter schools than regular public schools — does not apply to black students. In California, 81% of all socioeconomically disadvantaged black primary school students are in schools where more than half of the students are socioeconomically disadvantaged, but in charter schools 87% of socioeconomically disadvantaged black primary school students are in such schools, so they are probably more racially segregated as well.

When charter school supporters have noted the increased segregation that results from greater school choice, they have emphasized that black families tend to choose schools that have more black students. This type of segregation (as in Illinois) seems more benign to most observers. But segregation from choice also results from white families tending to choose schools with fewer black students. This type of segregation (as in North Carolina) more obviously conflicts with progress towards an integrated society.

The possibility of increased segregation is one of the costs policy makers should consider in evaluating charter schools' impact. In other words, charter schools could be causing harm even if their achievement were neither better nor worse than that of regular public schools. There might also be benefits from charter schools regardless of their impact on achievement (for example, parental sovereignty and/or choice, to some charter school supporters, is a desirable end in itself), but all costs and benefits should be considered, and increased segregation is apparently one.

The Hoxby studies

In two recent papers, Caroline Hoxby (a Harvard economist and signer of the *New York Times* advertisement) claims to show that students in charter schools do significantly better than students in traditional public schools (Hoxby 2004a, 2004b). She used a dataset that included 99% of students who attend charter elementary schools nationwide and compared, state by state, the average fourth-grade reading and math proficiency rates in these charter schools to those scores in the nearest public school or, alternatively, to those in the nearest public school with a similar racial composition. In some states she did not have fourth-grade data, so she used third- or fifth-grade data.

We here pay particular attention to these Hoxby studies because the first of them was apparently rushed to publication in September to refute the AFT's report that NAEP scores showed no higher achievement in charter than in regular public schools. This first Hoxby report was widely claimed by zealous charter school advocates as being a higher-quality study than the AFT's, because Hoxby claimed a near-universal sample of elementary students in charter schools nationwide, whereas the NAEP sample included only 3% of charter schools.[53] Chester E. Finn Jr. (2004d), for example, stated that "Hoxby has just issued the most effective rejoinder to the misleading AFT 'study' of charter school achievement…: she's done a far better study."

The Hoxby (2004a) study concluded that:

Charter school students are 3.8 percent more likely to be proficient on their state's reading examination when compared to students in the nearest public school. They are 4.9 percent more likely . . . when compared to students in the nearest public school with a similar racial composition....The average charter school student in the United States benefits from having a charter school alternative.

For example, in the District of Columbia, where about 17% of fourth-graders attend charter schools, Hoxby reported (2004b) that the share of charter school students who scored at or above proficiency in reading was 12% higher than the share of traditional public school students who did so. For math proficiency, it was 13% higher in charter schools. However, in the states that have the nation's largest charter school student populations — Arizona, California, Florida, Michigan, and Texas — totaling 60% of all charter school students, the charter school advantage was more modest and, in two of the cases, Texas and Michigan, it was zero or negative.[54]

Hoxby also argued that the difference in the proficiency proportion between charter and regular public schools increased as the age of charter schools increased. Thus, she estimated that if a charter school has operated for more than nine years, 10% additional students score at or above the proficiency level in both subjects; if it has been operating for five to eight years, 5% additional charter school students score above proficiency in reading and 4% more score above proficiency in math; if it has been operating for one to four years, 3% additional charter school students score above proficiency in reading (Hoxby 2004b).

There are a number of reasons why Hoxby's conclusions should be viewed with some skepticism:

In an important respect, Hoxby's studies violate the standards for educational evaluation set forth in the New York Times *advertisement she had recently signed.* She makes the comparison for only one year, 2002-03, and has no information about student gains from third to fourth grade. Second, before publication, her study was not "vetted by independent scholars."

Although Hoxby does have a large sample of charter schools, she has weaker measures of performance than the NAEP data. Hoxby used math and reading proficiency levels on individual state tests rather than the shares exceeding three levels of performance as in the AFT study (at or above basic, proficient, or advanced) and Hoxby does not have a measure of the average test score, which is available in the NAEP and used by the AFT. This means that information on how well students are doing, beyond whether they are above or below an arbitrary proficiency cut-point (one that varies from state to state), is not taken into account in her measure. For example, schools in which many students are just barely below the proficiency mark have higher performance levels than schools in which many students are far below that mark, although in Hoxby's analysis the schools are indistinguishable. In contrast, average test scores incorporate information on all students. In short, compared to the AFT's and NCES's NAEP analyses, Hoxby's greater sample size allows her to make a more precise assessment of a weaker set of performance measures.

Hoxby's point-in-time analysis provides an inadequate control for student characteristics or, at best, an unsubstantiated technique for this control. Hoxby's method is to compare the proficiency levels in charter schools to levels in the nearest school or to levels in the nearest one with a similar racial composition. This is an appropriate control for student characteristics only to the extent that charter schools and nearby public schools are demographically similar. For dense urban or suburban areas, this method could easily result in an inaccurate matching of student populations. As noted above (see p. 50), an independent analysis of Hoxby's database finds that, in fact, charter schools in her sample have more black but fewer Hispanic students and fewer lunch-eligible students than do the matched regular public schools (Roy 2005).

Surprisingly, Hoxby presents no tabulations of demographic characteristics to provide confidence in her methodology. The only controls she includes are whether the school targets at-risk students (91 schools of more than 1,100 schools in her study) or gifted students (three of more than 1,100 schools). Many more data about demographics could have been provided. For instance, how similar are the racial compositions? What are the differences in lunch eligibility? In urban and suburban areas, students in a charter school could be drawn from many regular public schools in its neighborhood, or even from several school districts, and many of these regular schools and school districts might be significantly different demographically from the one used as Hoxby's comparison.[55] Note that in Table 4, describing regular public schools in the KIPP-Bronx neighborhood, the average distance from KIPP of the four regular public schools identified as being those from which more KIPP students originated is nearly one mile; there are four other schools in the neighborhood that are closer to KIPP than three of these four sending schools; and Jonas Bronck Elementary School, the neighborhood school most nearly identical to KIPP demographically, is not a major source of KIPP students. **Table 10**, describing neighboring schools and those from which KIPP-D.C. draws students, shows that most of the schools sending significant numbers of students to KIPP are not in KIPP's immediate neighborhood but rather are more than two and as far as 7.5 miles away.

John Witte et al. (2004) show that in Wisconsin, with an inter-district open enrollment policy, charter schools in five mid-size school districts drew children from a number of surrounding school districts. At least in this state, the nearest public school may be the source only of a small proportion of students enrolled in a charter school. Indeed, Hoxby herself, in her analysis of three charter schools in Chicago (Hoxby and Rockoff 2004) shows that students in two of the charter schools travel, on average, two and five miles, respectively, to attend the schools. Comparisons with the nearest public schools in those two cases could give highly biased student performance comparisons.

Hoxby's choice of the nearest public schools (or nearest racially similar public schools) as a comparison group for charter schools also seems unjustified when considered in the context of charter school theory. Charter schools are designed to succeed because they have a more focused mission than regular public schools and therefore attract parents with a common philosophy. Charter schools are expected to differ widely from each other in approaches, permitting parents to choose the approach they prefer. By avoiding the heterogeneity of regular public schools, charter schools are also expected to avoid the conflict and confusion that arises when parents with widely differing philosophies are forced by school attendance boundaries to work together to make schools successful.

In *Charter Schools in Action* (2000), Chester E. Finn Jr., Bruno V. Manno, and Gregg Vanourek set forth this charter school philosophy (pp. 70-71):

Table 10. KIPP-DC Key Academy, distance from neighboring and feeder elementary schools (2002)

(a) Elementary school	(b) Distance from KIPP-DC (miles)*	(c) KIPP source schools a=main source b=sends a few students
Van Ness	0.3	
Tyler	0.6	
Watkins	0.8	
Bowen	0.9	
Brent	0.9	
Amidon	1.4	a
Maury	1.5	
Kenilworth	1.5	
Savoy	1.6	b
Payne	1.7	
Orr	1.8	
Birney	1.9	
Ludlow-Taylor	1.9	
Miner	1.9	
Thomson	1.9	
Randle Highlands	2.0	
Wilson, J.O.	2.0	
Moten	2.1	a
Stanton	2.4	a
King M L	4.0	a
Plummer	4.1	b
Malcolm X	4.2	a
Simon	4.4	a
Garfield	4.5	b
Shadd	4.6	b
Murch	7.5	b

* All schools that are located within 2 miles of KIPP-DC, plus other schools identified in column (c) as being source schools.

Sources:
b: Mapquest.com (because of one-way streets, some walking distances may be shorter).
c: Schaeffler 2004.

The charter idea recognizes that people differ along countless dimensions, from the loftiest (values, beliefs, and goals) to the most mundane (daily schedules and work lives)....The charter idea assumes that schools should differ from each other so that the diverse needs of a pluralistic society can be met....Not all children acquire skills and knowledge in the same ways or at the same rates. Not all thrive in the same settings. Not all have the same interests and needs. The reason to encourage schools to be different is so that all youngsters, not just those who blossom under the "one best system," will have the kinds of education that enable them to learn.

If this accurately describes what charter schools aim to do, then it makes no sense to judge their effectiveness by comparing them to the nearest (heterogeneous) public school that is attempting to accommodate the range of parent values, beliefs, and goals and the range of children's diverse ways of learning that exist in a single geographic community. One would need much higher levels of aggregation than a single school to make comparisons between charter and regular public school effectiveness.[56]

There is reason to be skeptical of Hoxby's findings because her conclusions about particular states are often in conflict with other research on those states:

- Hoxby's results for Arizona are contradicted by Solmon and Goldschmidt, who show more rapid increases for charter school scores but lower absolute scores in charter schools, even after the increases.

- Hoxby's conclusion that there is an overall test score advantage for charter school students nationwide is almost certainly overestimated because her California results disagree with the findings of other respected non-partisan studies of California charter schools (the RAND study, Loveless's charter school report, and Rogosa's estimates), all of which show that there is no significant difference in elementary school test scores between charter and regular public school students. Since charter school students in California comprise 22% of the total population of charter schools nationwide (California has the most charter school students of any state), an overestimate of the difference in that one state would reduce her estimated national reading and math proficiency advantage of charter school students to only 2% in math and 3% in reading.

- Hoxby's results for the District of Columbia are also at odds with those of Buckley, Schneider, and Shang (2004), who attempted to replicate Hoxby's findings using 2002-03 test score and demographic data from a variety of sources, and state (p. 4, note 2):

  Using both multiple and multivariate regression models controlling for demographic/programmatic factors, and various matching models on percentage of students eligible for free or reduced price lunch (similar to Hoxby's racial composition match but more relevant to D.C. given its demographics), we are unable to find any statistically significant evidence for a charter effect in achievement at any level of school (elementary, middle, or secondary). In fact, given several choices of model (including several matching approaches), we find evidence supporting [the AFT's] initial report that the traditional schools are outperforming their charter counterparts.

- Hoxby's results for Florida are contradicted by Sass, who shows that reading scores are no higher in charter schools than in public schools, and math scores are somewhat lower.

- Hoxby's results for Illinois are contradicted by Nelson and Miron (2002), who show that, on state tests, most charter schools in Illinois score lower than comparable schools in their districts.

- Hoxby's Michigan and Texas results accord approximately with those of the state studies that charter school achievement is not higher than that of regular public schools; her North Carolina results are negative for charter schools but much less negative than those shown by Bifulco and Ladd (2004).

Thus, in the five largest charter school states (Arizona, California, Florida, Michigan, and Texas), and for the largest urban charter school program, the District of Columbia, Hoxby's analysis does not suggest that students in charter schools do better.[57]

Hoxby's finding of a charter school advantage is not sustained when the data are controlled for students' demographic characteristics. When racial composition is controlled for directly, Hoxby's positive charter school effect for math proficiency disappears. When race and lunch-eligibility is controlled, the positive charter school effect disappears for both math and reading. Utilizing such controls, positive charter school effects disappear for charter schools in all locations: central cities, suburbs, large towns, and rural areas (Roy 2005).

The Hoxby studies may have further data problems. Hoxby issued two reports in late 2004. Although in the later one (2004b) Hoxby estimated, for the District of Columbia, a charter school fourth-grade proficiency advantage of 13% in math and 12% in reading, in the earlier report (2004a) these estimates were more than three times as large (40% in math and 37% in reading).

Following the issuance of Hoxby's first report, Howard Nelson (a co-author of the AFT report) obtained from Hoxby her District of Columbia data, and found several serious methodological flaws. He wrote (Mathews 2004[58]):

- Hoxby claimed that 100% of charter schools were studied, but only the nine charter schools authorized by the Public Charter School Board were studied while several others (those authorized by the [District of Columbia School Board]) were not included.

- Charter school proficiency was measured by NCLB proficiency standards (40th percentile) while the comparison school achievement was measured by the much higher proficiency standard used by the test maker (SAT-9).

- The combined results of the two large schools managed by the Edison Schools Inc., located in different parts of the city, were matched to only one neighborhood school.

- The nearest neighborhood schools in the Hoxby study almost always differed from the nearest school selected by greatschools.net or mapquest.com (frequently, several nearer schools were found with higher achievement).

Even when using Hoxby's lower-scoring comparison schools, merely adopting a common definition of proficiency — the one used for NCLB purposes [in calculating "adequate yearly progress"] — wipes out most of the 35 percent[age point] difference in [reading] proficiency favoring charter schools [and the 40 percentage point difference in math proficiency favoring charter schools]. Thus, both methods (NAEP and Hoxby's) yielded the same results for the District of Columbia — [approximately] no charter school effect.

Such errors are hard to avoid when researchers rush to publication before "vetting by independent scholars" in order to influence fast-moving policy debates.[59] Without a careful state-by-state examination of Hoxby's results, such as done by Howard Nelson for the District of Columbia, analysts should be cautious of additional possible errors in data collection and analysis for other states in the Hoxby analysis. Nelson himself reports having found such errors in an analysis of Hoxby's Illinois comparisons as well (Nelson and Miller 2004).

Summary of evidence on charter and regular public school achievement

In sum, the state-level studies, as well as NCES's own analysis, make the AFT report's inferences of poor charter school performance seem plausible, even though the NAEP data were only for a single year and the demographic controls were minimal. The state-level studies seem strongly to suggest that generally charter schools do not outperform regular public schools even when the charter schools have had time to mature and shake out early problems. When the strictest controls are used to correct for selection bias — that is, comparing the same student's performance in both charter and regular public schools, the effect on students of being in charter schools tends to be negative (at least in North Carolina). The most positive results for charter schools were found in Arizona in terms of more rapid gains for students in the early grades in charter schools, but these have not been found in other states. Since test scores in the Arizona charter schools sampled were so low initially, the greater increases in charter school test scores may have been the result of charter schools gaining experience (an age-of-school effect) and/or a possible effect of recovering from an unusually bad year for charter schools in the initial year of the sample used by Solmon and Goldschmidt (what statisticians refer to as "regression to the mean").

Thus, some studies do show positive gains for students in charter schools relative to students in regular public schools, but most do not. The studies indicate that charter schools contribute to greater school mobility, suggesting that "choice" may have negative as well as the usually expected positive effects on students and schools. And three of the studies indicate that, in states with significant black student populations, they are more likely to take advantage of charter schools than do other race or ethnic groups, but they and whites do so in a way that increases racial concentration in schools, inconsistent with the larger aims of integration and building common social values.

In one respect, the conclusions that charter schools do not systematically improve student achievement should have been expected, because they mirror conclusions from a study done of giving vouchers to attend private schools to low-income students in several cities. The study was performed by Paul Peterson (also a signer of *the New York Times* advertisement) and his colleagues (Howell and Peterson 2002) and demonstrated insignificant effects on achievement for typical low-income students. The authors found (and highlighted) positive achievement effects for a subset of black students, but the statistical methods they used to isolate this small subset are controversial (Krueger and Zhu 2004). Even if the Peterson team's methods are accepted, however, the positive effects are much smaller than voucher proponents predicted before the study results were published.

We asserted above that the best way to determine the true effect of charter schools was by means of a randomized experiment, but that such an experiment would be difficult to conduct for practical reasons. However, the Peterson voucher study was a randomized experiment, possible to conduct because a limited number of private scholarships were made available to finance the vouchers. When more low-income students applied than there were vouchers available, it became possible to randomize the assignment to voucher receipt.

Although charter schools and voucher plans are distinct policies, they have much in common. Both rely on a theory that regular public schools perform less well for disadvantaged students than would schools that were freed from bureaucratic regulations and union contracts typical of public school districts. And both emphasize the role of parental and student choice in creating competition between schools to succeed. That a true experiment would find little or no positive effect on student achievement for voucher plans is consistent with an expectation that charter schools would also produce little or no effect.

CHAPTER 6

The philosophy of charter schools

Are standardized test scores less important for charter schools, because charter schools will be shut down in any case if they don't perform well?

One claim made by charter school zealots, in response to the NAEP data on student achievement in charter schools, was that even though there are no standardized measures of gain scores by which a charter school's effectiveness could accurately be detected, this is not a serious problem because charter schools, unlike regular public schools, are shut down if their student performance is inadequate. As Howard Fuller (2004a) said, on behalf of the Charter Schools Leadership Council and in opposition to the *New York Times*' "misleading" report of charter school NAEP scores:

> While the vast majority of charter schools have provided disadvantaged children with superior education opportunities, in some instances, an individual charter school will not perform up to expectations. The strength of this movement is that low-performing charter schools have been and will be closed — fairly but swiftly. Unfortunately, we know that other low-performing public schools often go on forever.

Or, as Martin R. West put it: "Charter schools are also subject to regular review by their authorizers and, unlike traditional public schools, can be closed outright if their performance flags" (Mathews 2004). In response to the AFT's NAEP report, House Education Committee Chairman John Boehner (R-Ohio) asserted that, unlike regular public schools, charter schools can be closed down for low achievement: "Lobbying organizations such as the AFT and the so-called National Education

Association are spending millions to fight President Bush's efforts to make regular schools subject to similar accountability," he said (Soifer 2004).

The claim that charter schools' test scores are less important because, unlike regular public schools, charter schools have a built-in accountability mechanism in the threat of closure, and in the actuality of closure for poor performance, has been repeated often by charter school zealots. But the data indicate that charter schools are rarely closed for poor academic performance. When charter schools close, it is almost always because of financial mismanagement (they either go broke, or funds have been stolen by unscrupulous charter operators), not because of a failure to meet academic goals.

In October 2002, Jeanne Allen and the Center for Education Reform published a list of all charter schools that had been closed to that date, and the reasons for the closure (Allen and Looney 2002). As of that time, the center counted 2,874 charter schools that had ever opened. Of these, 154 had closed, as follows:

- 58 closures for financial reasons,

- 52 closures for mismanagement reasons,

- 8 closures for district reasons (for example, a district or state budget crisis forcing the closure of both regular and charter schools),

- 18 closures for facility reasons (for example, the inability to find or keep an adequate building for a charter school),

- 4 closures for "other" reasons (for example, charter schools that voluntarily closed because of infighting among the founders),

- 14 closures for academic reasons.

These 14 closures for academic reasons represent less than half of 1% of all charter schools. In view of the extensive data we have reported above showing that charter schools often post lower scores than demographically comparable regular schools, it is implausible that these 14 schools represent a significant proportion of low-performing charter schools that should be closed — "fairly but swiftly."

In one way, this conclusion may be unfair to the claims of the charter school zealots. If we accept the reasonable proposal that charter schools should be given at least three years before being held to account for academic performance, then these calculations should not include charter schools that were not already in existence at least three years before being considered mature enough to be subject to closure for academic reasons. If we adjust the center's calculations to include only such schools, the number that had been closed for academic reasons is still less than 1%.[60]

This is still a tiny number. Even if some charter schools enroll the most disadvantaged students who make big gains, yet have low-level scores, it is implausible that charter schools, on average, would simultaneously have low scores and be effective when so few ineffective charter schools were truly being closed for inadequate academic performance.

And it seems that the number of charter schools closed for academic reasons is even lower than the Center for Education Reform claims. Consider the case of charter schools in Arizona, second only to the District of Columbia in the proportion of its students who are in charter schools. The Center for Education Reform lists two Arizona charter schools that have been closed for academic shortcomings. But even these two cases do not illustrate that state or district regulators are closely monitoring charter schools and moving swiftly to close those that are low performing. One, the Community High School in Lake Havasu City, voluntarily returned its charter after only one year of operation, too short a time period for chartering authorities to evaluate test scores or other academic data (Jordison 2004). This voluntary closure does not illustrate "regular review" leading to closure if performance flags.

The other, the Real Life Charter School in Camp Verde, was indeed closed by its authorizer, the Peach Springs Unified School District. Taking advantage of Arizona's loose charter school regulations, this district issues charters to schools throughout the state of Arizona.[61] In the case of the Real Life Charter School (located 169 miles from the district office), academic concerns were not among the reasons for closure. Instead, the district took action because the school's chief executive officer simply abandoned the Real Life School. Most of the school's board members had also terminated their association. Enrollment had fallen below 10 students; its faculty consisted of a secretary who doubled as a teacher, and a fundraiser who doubled as a "curriculum specialist" (Parker 2001; Edwards 2001). Although the school may also have had academic shortcomings, it was the virtual collapse of the school that caused revocation of its charter. **Exhibit B** (Edwards 2001) is an affidavit from the office of the superin-

Exhibit B. Affidavit of district school superintendent regarding closure of Real Life Charter School, Tempe Verde, Ariz.

June 7, 2001

My name is Leah Edwards and I am the Administrative Assistant to the Superintendent at Peach Springs Unified School District. I assist my supervisor, Herman Parker, Superintendent, with the administration and oversight of the charter schools all over the state of Arizona.

Peach Springs issued a 90-Day Letter of Proposed Revocation to Real Life Charter School in Camp Verde Arizona with a hearing date of June 14, 2001. I am going to address the reasons for the letter.

1. Jim Richard has moved from the state and is no longer responsible for any facet of Real Life Charter School. He seemed willing to "sign the charter over" to a local charter school director who declined the favor.

2. The staff of the school consisted of a secretary/teacher and a part-time grants/curriculum person. Required state reports were not submitted on time. Calendar days were changed and not approved by the board. Most of the board members were no longer associated with the school and board-meetings were non-existent. When board minutes were requested, they appeared to be newly manufactured and no motions were made, seconded, voted upon or passed. The minutes consisted of finger pointing and tattling. We met with Cindy Earl, the grants/curriculum person in Cottonwood at ABS to explain their options and what must happen to continue. When these suggestions were ignored, we issued the 90-day letter of revocation. I contacted Jim Richard approximately 2 weeks ago and he told me he would "tender the charter" and send me an official letter ASAP.

In my opinion, Real Life Charter School is no longer a viable school.

Sincerely,

Leah Edwards

Notarized

tendent of the Peach Springs district, certifying this decision.

We investigated "academic closures" in Arizona only because it is the state with the largest share of students in charter schools. Although we did not conduct a similar case-by-case investigation of closures in other states, the Arizona experience, to the extent it is typical, suggests that few if any charter schools are being held accountable for academic achievement in any meaningful sense.

The low average scores of charter schools suggest that, if there are excellent charter schools that provide better educations for students than the regular public schools from which students came (and we have no reason to doubt that this is the case), there are also many ineffective charter schools that provide worse educations for students than did their regular public schools. In average data on charter school performance, the better and worse schools may offset each other. The NAEP data strongly suggest, but do not prove, that most of the ineffective charter schools are not being closed, even after their academic shortcomings have become obvious.

This suggestion is further confirmed in the U.S. Department of Education's most recent evaluation of charter schools (Finnigan et al. 2004). More than half of the surveyed authorizers reported having difficulty closing a charter school that was failing. In fact, charter school authorizers rarely used their power to implement formal sanctions (revocation and non-renewal); only 12% of authorizers had ever revoked a charter or denied a renewal (Finnigan et al. 2004, 47). Moreover, in the few instances when a formal sanction was implemented, authorizers most often cited reasons other than academic performance. Authorizers were more likely to issue a revocation or deny a renewal for issues of non-compliance with state and federal regulations or financial issues. Clearly, authorizers are struggling with accountability and seem unable to act "fairly but swiftly" as promised by the charter school zealots.

This conclusion is also consistent with that of a recent report published by the Thomas B. Fordham Institute (Palmer and Gau 2003; also summarized in Palmer and Gau 2005), a group that promotes charter schools and that is headed by Chester E. Finn Jr. (who is credited with assistance in the research design and writing of the report). It concludes:

The initial charter-school "promise" offered results-based accountability in exchange for freedom from excess paperwork and compliance monitoring. Unfortunately, this does not appear to be what's happening....This problem may be driven in part by state charter laws themselves (some of which don't allow much freedom to begin with), but much arises from the authorizers themselves as they struggle with accountability issues.

These data indicate that many authorizers are not doing an acceptable job of balancing accountability with flexibility. Either they are not being rigorous enough about results or their practices over-emphasize compliance.

In his forward to the Fordham report, Chester E. Finn Jr. insists that it would be wrong to conclude that charter school performance is poor from the fact that the charter school authorization and accountability system is not working well. Logically, he is correct. But in charter school theory, it is accountability for results (as opposed to compliance with procedures) that is supposed to guarantee superior performance. In view of the conclusion by these charter school supporters themselves that the charter school accountability system is ineffective, all that is surprising is that they would themselves resist data implying that, on average, charter school performance is poor.

Just as institutional inertia protects low-performing regular public schools from having to reform their approaches, the same institutional inertia protects low-performing charter schools from reform or closure. Charter schools often enjoy the support of organized political, parental, and community forces, and it is much easier for state and district officials to ignore their poor performance than to intervene and provoke unwelcome controversy.[62] The insistence of charter school zealots that the NAEP data did not reveal real problems avoids addressing the failure to hold charter schools accountable, in view of the inevitable barriers to such accountability that exist in a democratic political environment.

Some charter school supporters responded to the AFT's initial NAEP report on charter school achievement by acknowledging that greater monitoring of charter schools is necessary so that low-performing charter schools do not pull down the average achievement of charter students and thus discredit the entire charter school idea. Deputy Secretary of Education Nina Rees, for example, in response to the AFT's report, said: "We need to do a better job of monitoring these schools. I think the authorizers need to do a far better job....I think the states need to do a better job of monitoring how well the charter schools are doing" (Ifill 2004). In response to an earlier AFT report that was critical of charter schools, a bulletin published by Andrew Rotherham said, the "AFT is right that some charter schools under-perform, that some states have done a lousy job holding schools accountable, and that all publicly funded schools, including charter schools, need to be held accountable for academic standards" (PPI 2002). And Chester E. Finn Jr. has recently warned that the credibility of charter schools is being threatened by the failure of charter school authorizers to take accountability for academic outcomes seriously (Finn 2005).

Nonetheless, many zealous charter school advocates denounce any efforts to impose practical academic accountability regulations on charter schools beyond the right of parents to leave schools with which they are dissatisfied, and the theoretical obligation of states (rarely, as we have seen, fulfilled) to close schools that are not academically successful. Some charter school zealots have published reports that rank states by whether their chartering laws are strong (anything goes), considered good laws, or weak (with restrictions), considered bad (Finn, Manno, and Vanourek 2000; Allen and Marcucio 2004). If a state, for example, proposes to permit local school boards to examine a charter school design before granting a charter, to ensure that the school has a serious and credible plan to raise student achievement, or if a state requires waivers from regulations to be negotiated individually, rather than granted automatically, these charter school zealots have considered such policies to be a betrayal of the charter school principle. Yet given the poor track record of states and districts in closing ineffective charter schools once they are opened, it is hard to see how underperformance can be prevented without some additional regulatory oversight.

Many charter school supporters have not resolved their own theoretical conflicts about whether market forces (parent choices) are sufficient regulatory mechanisms, or whether states should ensure that charter schools really do operate in ways that are likely to, and in fact do, raise student achievement. And this conflict, in turn, reflects (and, in some ways distorts) a deeper philosophical ambivalence that runs through the charter school movement. Are charter schools intended to give parents the ability to choose their own goals for their children, whatever those goals might be, or should the public insist that public money be spent and charters granted only for the purpose of pursuing the public's goal of higher student achievement? If the purpose of charter schools is the former, then it really shouldn't matter whether NAEP scores, or any other measure, indicate that average charter school performance is lower; if parents feel more comfortable in schools that produce low achievement, they should be permitted to enroll their children in them.

Further, charter school proponents who hold this view should not only be concerned about comparisons using NAEP scores, but should also protest the No Child Left Behind law and its adoption of national requirements for minimal academic sufficiency, even if the technical flaws in NCLB's accountability mechanisms were corrected. If parental choice were a sufficient guarantee of school quality, then any regular public school in a district with open enrollment policies should be exempt from further accountability.

Are bureaucratic regulations and union rules the cause of low student achievement?

Based on data available, from NAEP and from state-level tests, it is impossible to assert that charter schools overall are doing a good job, with respect to test scores, as alternatives to regular public schools. Existing data strongly suggest that charter schools do not typically enroll children, particularly black children, who are more disadvantaged than students with superficially similar demographic characteristics in regular public schools. And the data strongly suggest that these charter school students do not post higher achievement than they would have done had they remained in regular public schools.

Evidence to the contrary primarily consists of anecdotes regarding a few charter schools that may not be representative of all charter schools serving disadvantaged children.

To understand why differences in achievement among disadvantaged students in charter and traditional public schools are probably negligible in most states, and favor public schools in some, it is helpful to review the theory underlying charter schools, a theory that was discussed more frequently when charter schools were first proposed than it is today. That theory was that student performance in regular public schools is inadequate, especially for the most disadvantaged students, because teacher union contracts and school district bureaucratic procedures prevent dedicated, creative, and innovative school leaders from developing new and more effective ways of running schools and teaching children. Freed from the constraints of bureaucratic rules and union contracts, schools can teach better and children can learn more. Howard Fuller says that charter schools and other alternatives to regular public schools exist for the purpose of "empowering the people to fight the bureaucracy" (Fuller et al. 2003). Chester E. Finn Jr. and his colleagues argue that charter schools stand in contrast to the regular public school system where good teaching and creative practices require "bureaucratic end-runs, often blocked by provisions of the union master contract and other special interests" (Finn, Manno, and Vanourek 2000, 59). As Jeanne Allen (2004b) recently put it:

> Free of bureaucratic and regulatory micro-management, charter schools can design and deliver programs tailored to educational excellence and community needs. Charters offer at-risk programs and state-of-the-art education. In charter schools, you'll find teachers that are there because they want to be, because they have more authority over the programs and approaches they use than they did in all their years in traditional public schools.

and CER (2004e):

> Charter schools are known to attract high-quality teachers who are solely dedicated to the best interests of their students. Because charters aren't bogged down by endless bureaucracy and politics, the teachers can do what they came to do — teach.

If, however, charter schools are not improving the achievement of disadvantaged children, it may be that the cause of low student performance is not bureaucratic rules but something else. When a treatment is based on a diagnosis, and the treatment doesn't work, it is prudent to examine not only whether the treatment should be improved, but also whether the diagnosis might be flawed.

The flaw in the theory that bureaucratic rules in regular public school systems are the primary cause of low achievement stems from a failure on the part of charter school proponents to distinguish between exceptional or anecdotal experiences and the typical experiences of schools overall. It is probably the case that the most creative and effective school leaders are stymied by bureaucratic regulations and union contracts, and that, freed from these rigidities, these creative and effective leaders can design excellent schools that do a better job of educating disadvantaged children than do typical regular public schools. This is why there are many examples of excellent charter schools, cited by charter school zealots as though they were typical.

But charter school zealots stumble by failing to understand that bureaucratic regulations and union rules do not exist for the purpose of suppressing creative practices. They exist primarily for the purpose of preventing corrupt, incompetent, and ineffective practices. Freed from bureaucratic regulations and union rules, many of the best educators can design excellent charter schools. But freed from these rules, many of the worst educators can also design terrible schools.

Financial management is one area where this has become clear. Many school districts have become notorious for their bureaucratic mazes, but almost every rule can be traced to earlier reforms to curb corruption. Because purchasing department employees were once caught in kickback schemes, districts now require multiple signatures and reviews of major purchases. Administrators and clerks verify orders, double-check prices, and audit inventories. School principals in regular public schools often complain that they can't fire janitors whose work is mediocre, but it is also nearly impossible for them to hire cousins or in-laws for maintenance positions. At one time, hiring relatives was routine in public employment. That's why it's now governed by cumbersome civil service rules.

Charter schools are designed to avoid these rules and thus to enable school principals to hire the most qualified people and to purchase supplies quickly and at low cost. As a result, many charter schools can theoretically function more efficiently than regular public schools. Some charter schools spend their funds in creative ways that would be prohibited in the public school bureaucracy — one of the most widely noticed strategies, adopted by both KIPP and the Edison Schools, is to hire younger teachers to work longer hours than regular public school teachers. The charter schools can pay these teachers more than young teachers in regular schools, but less than typical teachers in regular schools, at the same overall teacher payroll cost. The strategy requires that many teachers leave as they mature, but if a charter school can continue to attract young enthusiastic teachers who are inspired by the challenge, the strategy can be cost-effective. It remains to be seen how long KIPP and Edison can sustain this approach, but there is no evidence to date that it has failed.

But it is also inevitable that many charter schools, freed from bureaucratic rules that are designed to ensure a minimum level of competence, will develop approaches that are ineffective. This may be illustrated by the finding we reported earlier regarding California charter schools: those employing an outside-the-classroom curriculum do consistently worse in both reading and math tests than all classroom-based schools, whether they are other charter schools or regular public schools.

Some charter schools, freed from bureaucratic rules, will be tainted by corruption and mismanagement, cronyism and nepotism. Note that, while the Center for Education Reform's survey found that fewer than 1% of charter schools had been closed for academic shortcomings, over seven times that many had been closed for financial or other mismanagement.[63] Freedom from bureaucratic rules permits some charter schools to be unusually creative and others to be corrupt or inefficient. Charter school zealots focus their anecdotal accounts on the creative schools, but there is no evidence to date that charter schools, on the whole, are more efficient than regular public schools.

The ineffectiveness, on average, of charter schools may be due partly to these schools having hired at least as many, if not more, below-average as above-average teachers — although they have certainly hired some of the latter. Many charter school supporters have seized upon evidence that teachers are more effective if they had attended more selective colleges, themselves had higher test scores, or had more college coursework in the subjects they were teaching — although the latter finding has been confirmed only for secondary school math and science teachers (Ricc 2003). The charter school supporters have concluded from this that charter schools could outperform regular public schools if they were freed from state teacher certification requirements and could hire teachers without formal training in education but who had high test scores themselves and who graduated from more selective colleges.

This conclusion may be correct. Such charter schools may outperform regular public schools. The problem with this approach is that, while some charter schools will hire more qualified teachers if freed from state teacher certification requirements, other charter schools will hire less qualified teachers. Charter schools are unlikely to post high performance if their teachers have neither high test scores and selective baccalaureates, nor the pedagogical training, background in child development, and supervised practice that traditionally certified young teachers possess. When regulations requiring traditional certification are waived for charter schools, some charter schools will hire better-than-typical teachers and some will hire worse-than-typical teachers.

In fact, data from the federal government's 1999 Schools and Staffing Survey (SASS) show that, on average, charter schools had probably not hired more qualified teachers by that year. As **Table 11** shows, charter schools were slightly more likely to hire teachers who had graduated from the most selective colleges (14% of charter school teachers vs. 10% of regular public school teachers), suggesting that charter school teachers were more qualified on average by this measure. But on other available measures, charter school teachers seem to be less qualified. For example, in all types of communities sampled by SASS, charter schools were less likely to hire certified teachers. Overall, 93% of regular public school teachers were certified compared to only 72% of charter school teachers.

Some charter school supporters have argued that certification is a barrier to hiring teachers with extensive backgrounds in their fields of study, specifically teachers who have majors or minors in their subject areas, and that freeing charter schools from certification requirements permits such schools to hire teachers who are more qualified in this way. The SASS data, however, do not confirm this expectation. In mathematics, charter schools were less likely to hire teachers with extensive mathematics backgrounds. At the secondary level, where content knowledge is especially important, only 56% of charter school math teachers had extensive content knowledge in mathematics, compared to 70% of regular public school teachers.

For science, charter schools and regular public schools overall hired nearly the same percentage of teachers with a major or minor in science. Charter schools did hire more elementary school science teachers who had extensive content knowledge. But this did not hold for the secondary level, where 78% of regular public school teachers had college majors or minors in science, compared to only 67% of charter school teachers.

On average, teachers typically gain in effectiveness as they gain in experience, up to about five years of experience — although a few stud-

Table 11. Qualifications of charter school vs. regular public school teachers

	Charter schools	Regular public schools	Difference, charter schools vs. regular public schools
Percent of teachers who graduated from the most selective or highly selective colleges			
All Teachers	14	10	4
Percent of teachers with certification			
All schools	72	93	-21
Central city schools	65	93	-27
Urban fringe/large towns	78	94	-15
Rural/small town	78	94	-16
Elementary	76	93	-17
Secondary	66	94	-28
Percent of math teachers with college majors/minors in mathematics			
All teachers	39	51	-13
Central city schools	42	51	-9
Urban fringe/large towns	34	52	-18
Rural/small town	38	49	-12
Elementary	28	27	1
Secondary	56	70	-15
Percent of science teachers with college majors/minors in science			
All teachers	61	60	0
Central city schools	64	58	5
Urban fringe/large towns	56	63	-7
Rural/small town	68	58	10
Elementary	52	34	18
Secondary	67	78	-11
Percent of teachers with more than 5 years of experience			
All teachers	39	75	-36
Central city schools	34	75	-41
Urban fringe/large towns	40	73	-33
Rural/small town	53	77	-24
Elementary	38	74	-36
Secondary	42	75	-33

Source: Burian-Fitzgerald, Luekens, and Strizek 2004.

ies find effects of experience that end earlier or later than five years (Rice 2003). The SASS data show that charter schools have less effective teachers, measured in this way. About twice the proportion of charter school teachers as regular public school teachers had five years' experience or less in 1999. Not only is this a problem because of the inferior instruction that teachers who lack sufficient experience may deliver; the high concentration of inexperienced teachers in charter schools also deprives these teachers of opportunities for mentoring by more experienced teachers, one of the most effective ways in which teachers typically gain skill (Burian-Fitzgerald, Luekens, and Strizek 2004).

Low average experience for charter school teachers could be a result of the fact that charter schools are new, and so tend to hire younger teachers. But it also could be due to the fact that many charter schools try to keep their expenses low by purposefully hiring mostly young teachers, and then replacing them when these teachers have enough experience to feel entitled to higher salaries. As we noted above, this is explicitly the strategy of some highly regarded charter schools, such as the Edison Schools.

In sum, while freedom from certification rules undoubtedly permit charter schools to hire teachers who are more qualified than typical teachers in regular public schools, the data do not reveal evidence that charter schools, on average, are actually using their freedom to do so.

That data have shown, and will probably continue to show, no average differences in achievement between charter and regular public schools should have been no surprise to charter school supporters. That the charter process permits the establishment of schools that are both better and worse than regular public schools is frequently promoted as one of the charter school sector's strengths. As we noted above, some charter school supporters argue that charter schools should be evaluated mainly by whether parents are satisfied, not by objective measures of academic performance. As Chester E. Finn Jr. (2004a) wrote, in response to the AFT report:

> Some of the best schools I've ever been in are charter schools, some of which are blowing the lid off test scores in such vexed communities as Boston, New York and Chicago. And some of the worst — and flakiest — schools I've ever been in are charter schools. Yet people are choosing them.

If the best charter schools are equal in number (and in students served) to the "flaky" ones, we should expect charter schools' average results to be no better than those of regular public schools. If the "flaky" ones are more numerous, we should expect charter school results to be worse. There is no reason to assume that the number of good charter schools is greater than the number of bad ones.

The real question that charter school supporters should confront is not the question that the AFT's NAEP report stimulated — whether charter schools, on average, out-perform regular public schools — but rather whether the underperformance of some charter schools is a price worth paying for the overperformance of others. This is a much trickier public policy issue, and there is no easy answer to it.

Even this question may not fairly reflect the dilemma. The reaction of zealous charter school advocates to the AFT's NAEP report, and the expectation of these advocates that charter schools, on average, should outperform regular schools, reflects an unfortunate shift of some charter school advocacy from a pragmatic quest to identify school improvement strategies to an ideological prejudice against regular public schools. After all, an original motivation of the charter school movement was to spur experimentation that might discover better education models than those to which regular public schools are wed. But any true experimentation generates many failures until one or more successful models are discovered. If this is the case for charter school experimentation, we should expect charter schools, on average, to perform worse than regular public schools, even if charter school experimentation succeeded, eventually, in uncovering, through trial and error, better ways of doing things. An expectation that charter school performance, on average, should surpass that of regular public schools is tantamount to a claim that experimentation is not necessary because charter school operators already know what works. This view is inconsistent with the motivation of many early charter school proponents who were seeking new ideas for school improvement. Whether one accepts or rejects that approach (based on whether one believes that the harm done to children by the failures is outweighed by the possible good to be discovered in the event of successes), if the commitment to experimentation were implemented faithfully it is inevitable that charter schools, on average, will perform more poorly than regular public schools.

CHAPTER 7

Conclusion

What should we learn from the charter school dust-up of 2004? It may seem that the flurry of studies, news articles, and web postings that followed the AFT's August charter school NAEP report amounted to nothing more than partisans shouting past each other. This perspective, however, misses the important questions that have surfaced as a result of this debate, not only about charter schools but about what drives and how to judge school and student performance.

On the larger questions about schools, there are some important conclusions. First, evaluations of student achievement, whether in charter or regular public schools, cannot be made by examining test score levels without adequately taking differences in student characteristics into account. For fairness and accuracy, these characteristics need to be defined more precisely than simply race or ethnicity and lunch-eligibility. Moreover, evaluations of school performance also cannot be made by comparing changes from year to year in the level of achievement within the same school (or group of schools) because the comparison is for different student cohorts. A better, though not entirely flawless, way to evaluate school effectiveness is to account for the prior performance of students whose achievement levels are being observed.

Given these conclusions, which seem to be shared by charter school supporters and skeptics, it would seem necessary to change how schools are held accountable for performance in federal and state law, including the No Child Left Behind Act

Second, the claims made by many charter school supporters that charter schools would elicit sizable learning improvements, on average, because charter schools would be free of school bureaucracies and union contracts, has proven groundless. It seems that bureaucracy and union contracts have not been the cause of disadvantaged students' low performance, at least on average. Bureaucratic rules probably support as well as depress student achievement, just as the absence of these rules do. A completely unregulated environment can harm student achievement, just as an overly regulated environment can do so.

There are also important conclusions regarding charter schools themselves. First, the evidence available shows that charter schools do not generate higher average student achievement than do regular public schools and, especially, have not improved the educational performance of central city, low-income minority children. Second, charter schools do not typically enroll the "disadvantaged of the disadvantaged": rather, the minority students enrolled in charter schools are no more likely to be low-income than those in other public schools. Third, charter schools seem to be associated with some increased segregation in schooling. Fourth, charter schools churn students more frequently than regular public schools, and the achievement of students often suffers when they change schools. Fifth, charter schools, through the introduction of competition, are not systematically leading other public schools to be better.

It seems therefore that charter schools are not, and likely will not be, able to play a large role in reforming public education as a whole.

The failure of charter schools consistently to raise student achievement confronts school improvement efforts with an important ethical and policy dilemma. Even if some charter schools are excellent, and do a better job of educating children than do regular public schools, is this benefit worth the harm done by deregulation to children who are enrolled in charter schools that do a poorer job? We have not attempted to answer this question in this report, but believe that the charter school dust-up of 2004 should move it much higher on our common agenda.

Using different standards for evaluating charter and regular public schools

Following the publication of the AFT's analysis of charter school NAEP scores in August 2004, a number of Bush Administration officials and charter school zealots denounced both the AFT and the *New York Times'* coverage of the AFT report. These officials and advocates insisted that the coverage and report were improper because they failed to account properly for detailed student characteristics in the interpretation of test scores and because they failed to measure students' gains as opposed to score levels. The officials and advocates claimed that such errors could have been avoided if the AFT report had been independently reviewed before being published and if the *New York Times* had sought critical comments before writing about it.

These are reasonable criticisms but, as we noted in the main text of this volume, they are inconsistent with how these administration officials and charter school zealots typically analyze the performance of regular public schools. As we stated in the text, we review these inconsistencies here, not in an attempt to embarrass zealous charter school advocates but rather to challenge them to conform their views on the evaluation of charter and regular public schools to a consistent standard. That standard, we believe, should be one that conforms to the critiques they so appropriately made of the use of NAEP data to evaluate charter schools.

Statements made by administration officials and zealous charter school advocates are reviewed in turn:

Robert Lerner and the National Center for Education Statistics (NCES)

Results from the National Assessment of Educational Progress (NAEP) are regularly published by the National Center for Education Statistics (NCES) of the federal Department of Education, which refers to NAEP as "the nation's report card." As noted in the text of this volume, Robert Lerner, commissioner of Education Statistics until December 2004, said in response to the AFT's analysis that "[m]any factors affect student achievement, including socioeconomic status, race and ethnicity, and prior test scores. The current database does not account for these factors simultaneously. A more thorough analysis is needed to provide a statistically sound report, and we are working on one [for charter schools]" (Lerner 2004).

Mr. Lerner's call for a more thorough analysis was commendable, and much needed. However, when NCES finally did release its own analysis of charter school NAEP scores, there was no control for prior test scores, and no simultaneous accounting for the many factors that affect student achievement. That was not surprising; none of the numerous NAEP reports issued by NCES in the past 30 years has had any information about prior test scores.

Yet despite the failure of "the nation's report card" to include such controls, NAEP results are regularly used by government officials to prove that regular public schools are performing inadequately. NCES did not in fact develop a statistically sound (in Mr. Lerner's definition) report for charter schools, and has yet announced no plans to make NAEP's many other reports statistically sound in this sense. If a statistically sound report requires accounting for prior test scores simultaneously with other student background factors, major changes are required in how and what data NAEP reports — it would seem that NCES should now cease reporting NAEP scores without such simultaneous controls and that policy makers should cease drawing conclusions about school quality from NAEP results.

Indeed, as of this writing (more than five months after Mr. Lerner's letter calling for more statistically sound NAEP reports), the NAEP website continues to highlight comparisons based on NAEP scores that seem to imply conclusions which, by Mr. Lerner's current standard, seem unjustifiable. For example, the site compares NAEP scores from public and private schools and reports as "major findings" that "[I]n 2003, public-school students scored lower on average than non-public-school students at both grades 4 and 8" (NAEP 2004a). The website states that "[e]xamining these results reveals how these students [i.e., public and private school students] have performed in comparison to other groups in the year 2003 and whether they have improved" (NAEP 2004b). Nowhere on the NCES website is there a caution that the superiority of private schools cannot be inferred from such data, because, as Mr. Lerner's letter cautioned about charter schools, "many factors affect student achievement, including socioeconomic status, race and ethnicity, and prior test scores." Nowhere on the website does NCES explain how we can judge whether public or private schools have improved without information on the prior test scores of students who were in the fourth or eighth grade in 2003.[64]

Further, as many of the charter school supporters pointed out in their critique of the AFT report, each of the factors about which Mr. Lerner's letter cautioned interacts with the others; they cannot be considered separately.[65] Yet not only are data about prior test scores missing from NAEP reports, but only very sophisticated analysts can use NAEP data to perform analyses with multiple factors — for example, comparing how low-income black students in private schools perform relative to low-income black students in public schools. In NCES's summary pages for public use on the web, data are reported only for one category at a time: for blacks, for low-income students, for private school students. Such simple categories are of the kind that critics found inadequate when used to analyze charter schools.

NCES has continued, subsequent to Mr. Lerner's letter, to publish new conclusions about American education, based on NAEP, without any of the cautions that Mr. Lerner urged for the charter school data. For example, in October 2004, NCES published a pamphlet designed for popular use (it summarized data from a more detailed publication intended for specialists), the *Mini-Digest of Education Statistics* (NCES 2004a). The mini-digest included such conclusions as, for reading, "[s]eventeen year-olds scored about the same in 1999 as in 1973" (p. 28) and for math, "[f]or 17-year-old students, average performance had declined between 1973 and 1982, but an upturn during the past decade brought performance up above the 1973 level" (p. 29). Using the standards Mr. Lerner urged for charter school data, such reports of reading and math performance can be misleading without controls for socioeconomic status, race and ethnicity, and prior test scores. Nowhere in the October 2004 pamphlet does a reader find such cautions.

Former U.S. Secretary of Education Roderick Paige and Deputy Secretary Nina Rees

Reviewing the NAEP scores of regular public school fourth-graders, former U.S. Secretary of Education Rod Paige said that NAEP "is one of the best measures we have [and] will continue to be a critical tool, both in assessing our progress and in informing our decisions"; the scores show that "after spending $125 billion of Title I money over 25 years, we have virtually nothing to show for it" (Paige 2001a). Low NAEP scores of minority and urban children, he has concluded, are evidence that "our education system is broken and repair is needed urgently" (Paige 2001b). NAEP, however, "allows teachers, policymakers, and parents to identify problem areas and create strategies for improvement" (Paige 2001c). Yet when the AFT released its report on charter schools' NAEP scores, Secretary Paige said that the *"Times* made no distinction between students falling behind and students climbing out of the hole in which they found themselves. The *Times* grudgingly conceded that 'tracking students over time might present findings more favorable' to charter schools — but that point was buried at the end of the story" (Paige 2004). Deputy Secretary Nina Rees dismissed the possibility of drawing inferences from AFT's report, because "to draw any kind of conclusion about the benefits of charter schools needs…a longitudinal study using what we call randomized field tests" (Ifill 2004). Using such standards for the use of NAEP data, however, would make it impossible to know whether we have anything to show for the expenditure of Title 1 funds; disadvantaged children could be making great gains from kindergarten through the fourth grade, benefiting from Title 1 programs, and still have relatively low fourth-grade reading scores. Level scores from a single grade, without longitudinal information, cannot help teachers, policy makers, and parents to distinguish between students falling behind and students climbing out of the hole in which they found themselves.

Yet as Mr. Paige and his deputy certainly knew, the Department of Education consistently measures the effectiveness of schools without the benefit of longitudinal studies that are randomized field trials, and even without the benefit of non-experimental controlled longitudinal studies. No NAEP reports from the Department of Education have ever tracked students over time to see if this technique might present findings more favorable to regular public schools that serve the most disadvantaged students. Secretary Paige's statement went on to minimize the significance of low charter school scores, contending that "it is wrong to think of charter schools as a monolith. There are schools for dropouts, schools for students who've been expelled, schools serving the most economically disadvantaged families." Yet neither are public schools a monolith, but the secretary did not hesitate to use NAEP scores to judge the quality of public schools, notwithstanding the great variety in the types of students they enroll. NAEP has never been designed to break out data for "schools for dropouts, schools for students who've been expelled, [or] schools serving the most economically disadvantaged families."

In the months after the AFT's charter school NAEP report, Department of Education officials have had the opportunity to comment on other reports of student achievement, yet in no case of which we are aware were the standards the department announced for the AFT report resuscitated. In early December 2004, the department issued a press release announcing results of a comparative international test conducted by the Organization for Economic Cooperation and Development (USDOE 2004a). The release began:

> America's 15-year-olds performed below the international average in mathematics literacy and problem-solving, according to the latest results from the Program for International Student Assessment (PISA)....U.S. Secretary of Education Rod Paige said the results point to the need for reform of the nation's high schools. "The PISA results are a blinking warning light," he said. "It's more evidence that high standards and accountability for results are a good idea for all schools at all grade levels.

The press release concluded with a statement from NCES Commissioner Robert Lerner: "PISA provides important information about education in the United States and in other industrialized nations, giving us an external perspective on U.S. performance." No department spokespersons suggested that, without longitudinal data, such comparisons are inappropriate or that comparisons might be suspect if the relative social and economic disadvantage of students in different countries was not taken into account. In fact, PISA results showed that the social and economic composition of test takers explained a good part of the comparative disadvantage of which Mr. Paige complained: "white students performed above the OECD average in mathematics literacy and problem-solving, while Black and Hispanic students performed below the OECD average" (USDOE 2004a).

Several weeks later, also in December 2004, the department issued new results from the Third International Math and Science Survey (TIMSS). In this case, the department claimed that its reforms of recent years (the "No Child Left Behind" policies) had been proven successful by the fact that U.S. student scores were higher than in previous TIMSS administrations and higher than in other countries. But again, the department offered no caution that such comparisons might be invalid without demographic and longitudinal controls (USDOE 2004b).

In both cases, these international comparative test results were reported in *New York Times* articles, with sophistication (or lack of it) similar to that of the *Times* coverage of charter school NAEP scores the previous August. One was headlined, "U.S. Students Fare Badly in International Survey of Math Skills" (Norris 2004), the other, "Math and Science Tests Find 4th and 8th Graders in U.S. Still Lag Many Peers" (Arenson 2004). Neither Secretary Paige nor NCES officials protested this *Times* coverage and, needless to say, the signers of the *Times'* August protest advertisement did not take out another on these occasions.

Jeanne Allen and the Center for Education Reform

In 2003, the Center for Education Reform (sponsor of *The New York Times* advertisement denouncing the reporting of NAEP charter school results) was an aggressive proponent of a congressional proposal to finance private school vouchers and more charter schools in the District of Columbia, because of the what the center described as the District's "low quality public schools," illustrated by the fact that its test "scores are the lowest in the nation" (CER 2003). Yet in its *New York Times* advertisement, the center correctly argued that test scores cannot be used to judge the quality of charter schools because they do "not take into account such key characteristics of students known to affect their performance as parental education, household income, and the quality of learning resources in the home." In the District of Columbia these "key characteristics of students known to affect their performance" are considerably more disadvantageous than in the nation generally. One of Ms. Allen's critiques of the AFT study of NAEP charter school data is that "missing in the report was the fact that charter schools serve more poor, at-risk and minority students...." (Allen 2004a). Certainly the same consideration applies to evaluations of the District of Columbia's public schools.

Following the publication of Caroline Hoxby's (2004a) charter school study, CER issued a statement that "Hoxby's study goes a long way in providing quantifiable proof of widespread charter success." Yet the statement went on to acknowledge that, "like data from the National Assessment of Educational Progress (NAEP), the report does not examine individual student progress from year-to-year. That piece of the research puzzle must be completed to reveal the true extent of charter success" (CER 2004d). The center apparently believes that Hoxby's study goes a long way in providing quantifiable proof even though the center acknowledges that the study fails to meet standards it proposed, in the *New York Times* advertisement, should be required. This being the case, it is hard to see why the AFT study did not also go a long way in providing quantifiable proof.

Rev. Floyd Flake

As noted in the text of this volume, Rev. Floyd Flake wrote an op-ed article for the *Times* attacking the AFT study of charter school NAEP scores. Yet five years ago, Rev. Flake authored an op-ed article in the *New York Post*, supporting Florida Governor Jeb Bush's proposal to offer private school vouchers to students in Florida's two lowest-scoring schools, rescuing these children from what Rev. Flake called "the deadly waters of educational failure" (Flake 1999). This judgment of failure was based solely on low test scores, without controls for student background characteristics and without evaluating the gains that these students made from one year to the next. When NAEP data showed that charter school students' performance lags behind the performance of public school students, Rev. Flake dismissed the significance of this finding because the "charter students are much more likely to be non-white, eligible for free lunch programs, and residents of central cities." Conclusions that charter schools are not succeeding "ignores how much harder it is for schools with vastly higher percentages of poor and minority students to succeed," Rev. Flake argued. Yet in Florida five years earlier, the two regular public schools that Rev. Flake denounced had one of the most disadvantaged student bodies in the state, serving almost exclusively black students who resided in public housing projects in Pensacola.

In a speech given four years ago, Rev. Flake (2000) denounced:

> those who say that the problem has to do with the socioeconomic background of the child. To say that is to suggest that the child does not have the capability, the child does not have the will, the desire, the vision, the motivation, the determination to overcome socioeconomic barriers. If teachers believe that children cannot learn, they will teach in such a way that learning cannot possibly take place....If expectations are low, students will perform poorly, and they will not develop the competitive tools to function in this society.

In contrast, Rev. Flake then said, charter schools offer the best hope for preventing children's socioeconomic background from being used to justify low expectations. If this standard had remained central to the Rev. Flake's way of thinking, then the NAEP charter school scores would, to him, have been a damning indictment of charter schools.

Jay P. Greene, Kaleem Caire, and the Black Alliance for Educational Options

Jay P. Greene, a fellow of the Manhattan Institute, was also a signatory of the *New York Times* advertisement that insisted on the importance of assessing "carefully any research sponsored by interest groups engaged in policy debates. Such studies need to be vetted by independent scholars, as is commonly done in coverage of research on the biological and physical sciences." Yet two weeks after the advertisement's publication, Greene issued an unvetted report (co-authored with Greg Forster) on "teachability" trends. The Greene-Forster report (2004) stated that factors like poverty, social dysfunction, poor physical health, and economic insecurity (which the authors describe as indicating students' "teachability") can impact student achievement but "cannot serve as an excuse for the education system's failure to perform." Certainly the Manhattan Institute, sponsor of the Greene-Forster report, is an interest group engaged in policy debates, yet there is no evidence that the "teachability index" had been vetted by independent scholars. The acknowledgments section of the report mentions no such vetting. Indeed, the report suggests that Drs. Greene and Forster might only submit it at some later date to a peer-reviewed academic journal; its current publication, as a working paper, is intended, the authors say, to allow "other academics and the public to benefit from having the research available without unnecessary delay."

In an interview for *Education Week* magazine as his report on teachability was being released, Dr. Greene defended his practice of releasing unreviewed reports. The article describes Drs. Greene and Forster's aggressive public relations campaign for their report, including, for example, "[t]wo whiteboards on their office walls [that] lay out the timeline for sending follow-up e-mails" to reporters who had received copies of the teachability report in advance of its official release (Cavanagh 2004). The *Education Week* article said:

> While many education researchers follow the process of peer review — the practice of having others in the field critique one's work before publication — Greene contends that the benefits of that route are exaggerated. Those reviewers are themselves sometimes biased, he argues; they often add little to the accuracy or value of the study; and above all, the process is slow. He wants his office's work to speak to the relevant education issues of today — not those of two or more years ago.

When Dr. Greene was questioned by the *Education Week* writer about the apparent contradiction between this policy and the *New York Times* advertisement he had signed, Dr. Greene said that the advertisement shouldn't really be taken to mean that studies should be vetted by independent scholars; rather, it only meant that reporters should seek also to quote critics when writing about the studies. Yet that was exactly what *New York Times* reporter Diana Schemo had done when reporting on the AFT's charter school NAEP scores; in writing the article, she had interviewed (and the article quotes) three experts whom she had reason to believe would be most critical of the AFT's report — Jeanne Allen, Chester E. Finn Jr., and Robert Lerner.

As noted above, the *New York Times* advertisement stressed that parental education, family income, and home resources affect student performance, and claimed that proper consideration of such factors might show charter schools to be successful. Yet, Jay Greene, a signatory, had also previously produced high profile work that does not take student characteristics into account when studying student and school performance. Three years before, Dr. Greene authored a report for the Black Alliance for Educational Options, one of the charter school advocacy organizations on whose behalf Chester E. Finn, Jr. originally proposed that NAEP collect charter school data. This report (Greene 2001) concerned high school dropout rates, not test scores, but if background characteristics should be taken into account in evaluating test scores, these characteristics would influence dropout rates as well. The report presented state-by-state and city-by-city data on high school completion and presumed that differences in dropout rates reflect differences in school performance. Similarly, the report compared differences in high school completion by race within states without any consideration of other background characteristics that could explain the racial gaps. Dr. Greene's report bemoaned the fact that "the gap between white and minority graduation rates is alarmingly large," although he acknowledged that "this report does not consider why graduation rates are what they are" nor "explain why rates are lower for some areas or for some populations."

Nonetheless, Kaleem Caire, president of the Black Alliance for Educational Options, in his forward to the Greene report, wrote that "[r]eviewing the findings of this report — including the horrific graduation rates in such cities as Cleveland and Milwaukee — it is no wonder why parents there have led the fight for education vouchers and other new educational options for their children" (Greene 2001). Caire argued that the Greene report was needed because "[p]arents and other taxpayers must have accurate information about the educational status of our nation's children." Yet the Greene report suffers from all of the limitations inherent in the point-in-time analysis of NAEP test scores conducted by AFT researchers and, later, by NCES itself. The Black Alliance for Educational Options has frequently argued that public schools fail black children and has supported this argument by comparing white and black test scores without any consideration of other factors such as income and parental education status. In a newspaper advertisement, for instance, the organization noted that "test scores in the elementary schools in Atlanta's black neighborhoods are substantially worse than scores in public schools in majority white neighborhoods," and this is evidence of "a failing public [school] system" (BAEO 2002).

Howard Fuller

Howard Fuller, another signatory of the *New York Times* advertisement, is a professor at Marquette University, a former superintendent of schools in Milwaukee, and long a leading proponent of private and charter schools as alternatives to regular public schools for low-income black children. In his keynote address to a 2001 conference of charter school supporters, Dr. Fuller (2001) said that "the unwillingness or the inability of so many schools and school systems to educate [the poorest children of color] is not primarily a factor of their race or class." Dr. Fuller went on to warn his fellow charter school supporters against developing "a two-tiered way of looking at schools." He said that he worries when charter school supporters "make excuses and say things like, 'You know that we are dealing with the toughest kids here?'" Dr. Fuller reminded his fellow charter school supporters that:

> [W]e asked for those kids, because we were going to make it better for them. Now that we have them, why are we complaining? If we cannot do a better job with these children than the place that they came to us from, then we don't deserve to have them, and they should return to where they started. Why should we have these kids if we cannot do a better job than the system that we are criticizing? In the end, we must do a better job with kids that are very demanding of us.

Dr. Fuller's signing of the *Times* advertisement, with its suggestion that dealing with the toughest kids is a valid excuse for low test scores, indicated a clear shift in his standards. This was confirmed when, in October 2004, the Charter School Leadership Council (chaired by Dr. Fuller) issued another statement attacking both the AFT report and the *Times'* coverage of it (CSLC 2004). Asserting that the AFT report was flawed, the council asserted that:

> [T]he researchers were only able to control for one variable [i.e., student demographic characteristic] at a time rather than controlling for multiple variables, as is accepted practice for education

research....This is a significant issue...because it is well established that factors such as race play a role in student performance even when other variables are taken into account. For example, though researchers disagree about the cause, African-American students do not, on average, score as well on standardized tests as white students from similar socioeconomic backgrounds.

Nonetheless, almost contemporaneously with this Charter School Leadership Council statement, Dr. Fuller announced that "results from Professor Hoxby's comprehensive study on charter school student achievement demonstrate that charter schools are working for America's families, particularly low-income, minority families." Despite the lack of longitudinal data, and despite the failure of the Hoxby study to meet the criteria set forth in the Charter School Leadership Council statement, Dr. Fuller concluded that the Hoxby finding that "charter school students are more likely to be proficient in reading and math than the students in similar, nearby public schools" means that "[t]he lesson is clear: charter school students have higher achievement today than they would if their charter schools didn't exist" (Fuller 2004b).

"Shoot the Messenger" reactions of charter school zealots

Andrew Rotherham, director of the Progressive Policy Institute's education program and a zealous charter school advocate who had called the AFT study a "hatchet job," concluded that Hoxby's report was "much more sophisticated than the recent AFT report" (Rotherham 2004b). In actuality, Hoxby's report was not more sophisticated and, in fact, has less persuasive test score data: the only test score information Hoxby uses is the percent of students in charter and regular schools who passed state proficiency cut-points, whereas the AFT reported both on NAEP scale scores and proficiency levels. Both the Hoxby and AFT reports use the same, simple statistical technique of comparing differences relative to a standard error.

Rotherham contrasted the reliability of the AFT report with Hoxby's, saying "you should have about as much confidence in a charter school report from the AFT as you would in a military outsourcing report from Halliburton," whereas the Hoxby study, "[w]hile also limited in several ways in terms of what it can tell us...offers a more complete picture of charter performance" (Hendrie 2004).

Such attacks on the legitimacy of the AFT's charter school research were common to many charter school zealots' critiques of the NAEP charter school results. Such a "shoot-the-messenger" approach is particularly inappropriate in charter school debates, because many charter school research reports have been published by analysts who are previously on record regarding the policy advisability of charter school expansion or whose research is sponsored by advocacy groups with strong positions on the issue. Certainly, Hoxby should be no more immune from such criticism than the AFT; she is a member of the Hoover Institution's Koret Task Force on K-12 Education, whose members are at least as vociferous in their support for charter and private schools as the AFT is in opposition.

Two months after the release of the Hoxby report, the Department of Education released a study of charter schools, several years in the making, that found students in charter schools less likely to meet state standards than students in regular public schools. Again, the significance of these findings were dismissed by the same charter school zealots who had recently praised the Hoxby study, although both shared a common shortcoming with the AFT's NAEP report. A spokesman for the Charter School Leadership Council said that the Department of Education report "sheds no light on the actual performance of charter schools or the value they add to student learning" because it did not include measurements of the evolution of student achievement over several years at charter schools. "In this respect it probably clouds the picture rather than clarifies it" (Dillon and Schemo 2004).

Alternative presentations of NAEP charter school demographic data

As noted in the text of this volume, the data reported in Table 1 include only students who took the fourth-grade NAEP math exam and who reported whether they were or were not lunch-eligible. About 10% of charter school students and about 4% of regular public school students did not report whether they were eligible. We know of no plausible explanation for the difference in reporting rates between charter and regular public school students, and therefore have no basis for assigning non-reporters to the eligible or non-eligible category.

Table 1 assumes that non-reporting charter and regular public school students were or were not actually lunch-eligible in the same proportion as those in their respective school sectors who did report their eligibility.

Here we present two alternative ways of interpreting the data:

Table B-1 drops all non-reporting students from the sample. It shows the students who were or were not lunch-eligible as a share of all students who reported whether they were or were not eligible.

Table B-2 makes an assumption most favorable to charter school supporters. It assumes that the 10% of charter school students who did not report their eligibility were, in actuality, eligible for lunch subsidies. And it assumes that the 4% of regular public school students who did not report their eligibility were, in actuality, not eligible for lunch subsidies.

We provide interpretations of these tables on pages 35-36 of the text of this book.

Table B-1. Percent of students eligible for free or reduced-price lunch, by race and location

	Percent eligible for free or reduced-price lunch		
	Charter schools	Regular public schools	Difference
Total	42	44	-2
Central city	58	62	-4
Urban fringe	27	34	-7
Rural	20	40	-20
All blacks	61	74	-13
Central city	65	81	-16
Urban fringe	43	61	-19
Rural	78	73	5
All whites	20	26	-6
Central city	34	35	-1
Urban fringe	15	16	-1
Rural	12	26	-13
All Hispanics	67	74	-7
Central city	n/a	80	n/a
Urban fringe	n/a	67	n/a
Rural	n/a	75	n/a

Note: Data are for students who took the NAEP 4th Grade Math Assessment, including all those who reported their eligibility for free or reduced-price lunch and those who failed to report their eligibility

Source: NAEP 2005; supplemented by unpublished data furnished to the authors by the National Center for Education Statistics.

Table B-2. Percent of students eligible for free or reduced-price lunch, by race and location, assuming all non-reporting charter school students were eligible and all non-reporting regular public school students were not eligible

	Percent eligible for free or reduced-price lunch		
	Charter schools	Regular public schools	Difference
Total	52	44	8
Central city	68	62	6
Urban fringe	32	34	-2
Rural	53	40	13
All blacks	71	74	-2
Central city	75	81	-6
Urban fringe	55	61	-6
Rural	93	73	20
All whites	31	26	5
Central city	47	35	12
Urban fringe	18	16	2
Rural	44	26	18
All Hispanics	74	74	0
Central city	n/a	80	n/a
Urban fringe	n/a	67	n/a
Rural	n/a	75	n/a

Note: Data are for students who took the NAEP 4th Grade Math Assessment, including all those who reported their eligibility for free or reduced-price lunch and those who failed to report their eligibility. For charter schools, "eligible" students include those who reported they are eligible, plus those who failed to report. or regular public schools, "eligible" students include only those who reported they were eligible.

Source: NAEP 2005; supplemented by unpublished data furnished to the authors by the National Center for Education Statistics.

Endnotes

1.   Throughout this book, except where specifically noted otherwise, we refer to students who are eligible for free or reduced-price lunches as students who are eligible for lunch subsidies, who have lunch eligibility, or who are lunch-eligible. Students who are eligible for free lunches come from families with incomes no greater than 130% of the federal poverty line; students who are eligible for reduced-price lunches come from families with incomes no greater than 185% of the poverty line.

2.   Not all signers of the advertisement have been associated with zealous charter school advocacy, and at least two signers — David Figlio and James Heckman — subsequently removed their names from the advertisement when it was published elsewhere.

3.   Mr. Lerner was appointed by President Bush to head the National Center for Education Statistics on December 23, 2003 without Senate confirmation. Lerner's recess appointment expired when Congress adjourned in December 2004, and he no longer formerly held the office when NCES's own analysis of NAEP data was released. Instead, he was employed on a 120-day consulting contract, but believed the chances were "very good" that he would be renominated by the president to be commissioner (Davis 2005).

4.   In social science, a "Hawthorne effect" is the tendency of study subjects to behave differently when they know they are being studied than they behave normally.

5.   How different starting points can affect the potential for progress is an empirical question whose resolution is not obvious. It is plausible that children who start lower can make greater gains because the gaps in their learning are easier to fill. It is also plausible that children who start higher can make greater gains because academic success comes more easily to them, either because they have more natural ability or because they have better family support.

As Ballou (2002) has observed:

In effect, value-added assessment "controls for" the influence of family income, ethnicity, and other circumstances on students' initial level of achievement. However, this may not be enough. The same factors may influence not just the starting level, but also the rate of progress....

To practice value added assessment, we must be able to compare the achievement gains of different students in a meaningful way. We need to be assured that the scale on which we measure achievement is one of equal units....If it does not, we will end up drawing false conclusions about the relative effectiveness of these students' teachers and schools.

Mathematicians who specialize in measurement in the social sciences, together with ...psychometricians have devoted considerable attention to this matter. Their findings are highly unfavorable to value-added assessment....

...As Henry Braun of ETS wrote in a 1988 article for the *Journal of Educational Measurement*: "...we should probably give up trying to compare gains at different places on the scale for a given population."

6.   The term "gains" is used in two ways in education policy debates. Sometimes, it is used to compare the scores of two different cohorts; for example, if a school's (or the nation's) fourth-grade scores this year are higher than the same school's (or the nation's) fourth-grade scores in a previous year. Because such comparisons involve two different groups (cohorts) of children, the comparisons do not necessarily indicate better performance. For example, the later cohort may have had higher entering kindergarten abilities, so its higher fourth-grade scores may not indicate anything about the efficacy of schooling. Although this use of the term "gains" is commonplace, it is not properly used to describe such comparisons, and we do not use the term in this book to describe such differences in achievement between different cohorts.

The second and proper way to use the term "gains" is to refer to the actual learning that a single group of students accomplishes from one year to the next; for example, how much achievement increases when the same group of students moves from the third to the fourth grade.

However, even used in this proper way, there can be inaccuracies in the use of the term "gains." If the membership of a cohort changes from year to year, then comparisons of that cohort's fourth-grade scores with that cohort's third-grade scores the previous year may not truly reflect "gains" but only changes in the membership of the group. We usually use the term "gains" in this report to refer to changes in the average scores of a cohort from one time to another, but recognize that this may not always be entirely accurate. It is, however, far more likely to be accurate than using the term "gains" to describe differences between average scores in a single grade of successive cohorts.

7.   In this book, the term "selection bias" is used only in its technical sense — that for whatever reason, a group is chosen that is systematically unrepresentative of a larger group. The term "bias" does not imply that those who select students are discriminating in favor of or against some students, or that they are purposely attempting to choose an unrepresentative sample.

Analysts have developed several methods to deal with selection bias as represented by omitted variables. One way is to include student or school "fixed effects." When student outcomes are measured over time, fixed effects control for student characteristics that are invariant over time. For example, Rouse (1998) compared student performance in Milwaukee private voucher schools compared to students in public schools in the period 1991-94. She used student fixed effects to control for time invariant observable and unobservable student characteristics. Bifulco and Ladd (2004) also use fixed effects as an alternative to including observable student characteristics in regression estimates of charter/public school test score differences over a four-year period in North Carolina.

A second method to correct for omitted variables is to include an "instrumental variable" in the analysis (Angrist and Krueger 2001). An instrumental variable must have the property that it is correlated with the independent variable of interest but not with the dependent variable. For example, Angrist and Krueger (1991) used birth date and compulsory school laws (students cannot leave school before their 16th or 18th birthday, depending on the state) to estimate the effect of staying in school longer (those whose birthdays occur earlier stay in school longer) on earnings. Birth date is a good instrument because it determines who starts school in a given year or a year later, but it is not *a priori* related to an individual's ability, family resources, or other omitted variables that might influence earnings.

A third method used to correct for selection bias is propensity scores (Rosenbaum and Rubin 1983). Most regression analyses in non-randomized observational studies are carried out for the full range of a particular sample, without regard for the probability that individuals have of being in the treatment or control groups. Take the example of student performance in private compared to public schools. Students from disadvantaged families are much less likely to attend a private school than a public school. At the other end of the spectrum, students from well-off families, particularly minority high-income families, have a relatively high probability of attending a private school. To approach a random assignment trial, we should compare observations from our non-randomized survey of individuals that have a reasonable probability of choosing to be in the treatment or control group. The difference in their achievement scores would be closer to the difference we could expect in a random assignment of students to the two groups, since it is much more likely that their omitted characteristics are similar. Propensity scoring weights observations to reflect the probabilities that individuals could be in the treatment or control groups.

8.   A state whose own accountability system (Florida is one example) utilizes the more preferable "value-added" or gain score method must maintain two conflicting accountability systems — its own and the federal system of NCLB. This often leads to the absurd result that a school is deemed failing under one system and successful under the other.

9.   We say that it "may not" be possible for schools to eliminate gaps on their own because schools have never been able to do so and would not be able to do so even if current school improvement efforts were reasonably extrapolated. It is always theoretically possible that a newly discovered school improvement strategy would demonstrate that schools alone could eliminate achievement gaps. Schools can accomplish an *apparent* elimination of achievement gaps if they define gaps only by comparing the percentages of students from different groups who achieve "proficiency," and then define "proficiency" at a very low level. See Rothstein 2004.

10.   In describing the possibility of a new consensus, we do not discuss another flaw, not mentioned in the *New York Times* advertisement, in the current use of test scores for accountability purposes, i.e., the inaccuracy of single tests to measure fine distinctions in school performance. Recognition of the statistical "noisiness" of such tests should also be included in a new consensus. A particular problem is that gain scores are more subject to inaccuracy than point-in-time scores, because gain scores too optimistically assume the accuracy of each of two separate tests, not only one. For a discussion of the statistical problems that arise when test scores of any kind are used as the exclusive means of accountability, see Kane and Staiger (2002).

Nor do we discuss whether it is appropriate to hold any schools, charter or regular public, accountable solely for test scores, no matter how accurately these scores are measured. Regular public schools have many goals besides the basic academic skills that tests measure, and many charter schools have been established because parents and teachers believed that regular public schools were giving insufficient emphasis to some of these other goals.

11.   Cross-sectional analyses can certainly be useful, and we do not take the position that they should never be performed. Many things can be learned and some ideas proven wrong with cross-sections. But educational policy today relies too heavily on conclusions from cross-sectional data without the necessary cautions and qualifications. As this book demonstrates, the inferences drawn from the AFT's NAEP analysis are consistent with other evidence and identify important policy concerns.

12. This call for reform of NCLB may reflect a welcome change of position on the part of the authors, or a conflicted point of view. As recently as December 2003, Hess wrote an essay, posted on the website of the American Enterprise Institute, denouncing those who would placate critics of existing accountability systems by making compromises such as those called for in Finn and Hess (2004). Dismissing the kinds of objections he and Finn would later raise about NCLB as mere "warts," Hess wrote: "The important split is not between ideological proponents and opponents of accountability, but between those who support tough-minded accountability, despite all its warts, and those who like the ideal of accountability but shrink from its reality….The choice is between an imperfect accountability system and none at all" (Hess 2003).

13. This should not be taken as a suggestion that these regular public schools are not failing, but only that such judgments cannot be made using point-in-time score data. Recent research, especially that from the National Center for Education Statistics' "Early Childhood Longitudinal Survey," has shown that disadvantaged children enter kindergarten already far behind (Lee and Burkam 2002). This being the case, some regular public schools serving such children could have relatively low test scores but children in these schools could still be making great gains.

14. Although test scores of recent arrivals need not be counted in a state's calculations of a school's "adequate yearly progress," this concession does not account for the challenges posed to a school's instructional program by having rapid student turnover, nor does it account for the reality that a school's effectiveness in any grade does not only (or primarily) result from instruction in that grade but also from instruction in every previous grade. Even if students are present in a grade for an entire school year, their test scores in that year reflect the quality of instruction of schools where those students were educated in previous years.

15. The quotation is the *Times'* summary of Mr. Finn's previous position, and not a direct quotation from him.

16. For example, Rev. Floyd Flake was formerly the president of Edison Charter Schools. Deborah McGriff, wife of Howard Fuller, is currently a vice president of the Edison Company. John Chubb, co-author with Terry Moe of an influential 1990 book promoting private schools, and another outspoken critic of the AFT NAEP data, is the chief education officer of Edison.

17. It would not be unethical to conduct such experiments if there were no shortage of spaces or surplus of applicants. Medical trials deny treatments suspected of being beneficial to members of control groups, even when these controls could be administered the treatment. The ethical balance in such cases weighs the benefit to the more numerous group of future patients against the withholding of a possible benefit to some present patients. The same ethical considerations would apply in education experiments. However, as a practical political matter, it is easier to justify withholding admission to charter schools to those who lose in a lottery when there are insufficient places for all who apply.

18. It is possible to analyze differences between charter and regular public schools by gender, but because there are virtually no differences in gender distribution across the whole or even major subgroups of charter and public schools, gender distribution has

little effect on the results. However, as we show later (see pp. 60-62), because girls generally score higher in reading and somewhat lower in math, comparisons of smaller subgroups of charter schools with regular public schools can be influenced by the proportion of girls attending charter schools.

19. It may seem puzzling that charter schools overall have a slightly higher percentage of lunch-eligible students than regular public schools overall while at the same time each race or ethnic group has a lower percentage of lunch-eligible students in charter schools than in regular public schools. This counter-intuitive arithmetic paradox is due to the different race and ethnic compositions of charter schools and regular public schools. In particular, black students are represented more heavily in charter schools than in regular public schools (31% vs. 17%). It is also true that the share of lunch-eligible black students in charter schools is lower than the share of lunch-eligible black students in regular public schools (68% vs. 76%). Nevertheless, because the rate of lunch eligibility among black students is greater than average, the higher proportion of black students in charter schools raises the overall rate of lunch eligibility in charter schools. Charter schools also have fewer white and Hispanic students relative to regular public schools. The net effect of the differences in composition is that the overall rate of lunch eligibility in charter schools is slightly higher than that of regular public schools, despite a lower rate of eligibility within each race and ethnic group. Seeming arithmetic paradoxes like this are commonplace when component subgroups with differing weights are combined into wholes.

20. The AFT's (2004a) estimate of lunch-eligible students (54% in charter schools, 46% in regular public schools) differed from that of the National Center for Education Statistics (NAEP 2005) which reported that 42% of students in charter schools and 44% of students in regular public schools are eligible. (In both cases, these figures include both students who reported whether they were eligible plus those who did not report whether they were eligible in the denominator.) This difference between the AFT and the NCES estimates is attributable to differences in the weighting of subpopulations in the total sample. When the NAEP is administered, some minority populations are over-sampled in order to generate samples that are large enough to reduce the standard errors to acceptable levels. In its calculations, NCES adjusted for this over sampling. In August, however, when the AFT performed its analysis, the weights to be used for this correction were not available to the AFT or to other members of the public. Had the AFT had access to these weights, its methods would have resulted in an estimate that 44% of charter school students were lunch-eligible. The additional difference between this corrected AFT estimate of 44% and NCES's finding that 42% were eligible is attributable to NCES's reclassification, subsequent to August, of some [12] regular public schools as charter schools in the NAEP sample (Goldstein 2004).

A recent U.S. Department of Education report used the federal Schools and Staffing Survey (SASS) to estimate the percentage of students in charter and regular public schools by race, ethnicity, and lunch eligibility. It shows the percentage of black and Hispanic students in charter schools rising from 45% in 1998-99 to 57% in 2001-02, with the percentage of blacks rising substantially and the percentage of Hispanics declining slightly during this period (Finnigan et al. 2004, Appendix Table C-2, p. 83). These 2001-02 estimates are higher than the 51% of charter school students who are black (31%) or Hispanic (20%), according to the NAEP sample for 2003 (NAEP 2005, Table A-6). The Department of Education's estimates also show the percentage of charter students who receive lunch subsidies rising from 39% in 1998-99 to 53% in 2001-02 (Finnigan et al.

2004, Exhibit 3-7, p. 25). This estimate of the percentage of lunch-eligible charter school students in 2001-02 is also higher than the estimates from the NAEP sample for 2003, regardless of how those who did not report their eligibility are distributed (see Tables 1, B-1, and B-2 of this report). These discrepancies between the demographic estimates from SASS and from NAEP have not been explained. Officials at NCES speculate that the differences could be attributable to the SASS and NCES samples having been taken in different years; to the SASS data collection being taken at the school level while NAEP is a student-level sample; and to sampling error. Those "three differences could easily account for" the discrepancy (Goldstein 2005).

21.   Solmon and Goldschmidt (2004) do not measure students' socioeconomic background directly. They do use two proxy variables — "migrant" and "English not primary language" as controls in their regression analysis, but do not present comparisons for charter and regular public school students of the means of these variables.

22.   In its 2000 report (p. 32), the Colorado Department of Education states that half of the charter schools in the state did not offer a hot lunch. In its 2003 report (p. 21), this claim is less certain: the department still says that some charters did not offer hot lunches, but it places more emphasis on a suspicion that some charter schools may offer a lunch but not report the fact. The department says that 15 charter schools report 0% lunch-eligibility, and suspects that these schools simply did not collect or report the data. However, the department offers no evidence, anecdotal or otherwise, to support this suspicion. It acknowledges that charter schools that do not report the percentage of students who are eligible for the lunch program may fail to report because they do not offer a lunch program and so mistakenly believe that the reporting requirement does not apply to them. Charter schools that do not offer a lunch program are unlikely to be those serving socioeconomically disadvantaged children, and so considering "no-report" to be the same as "none eligible" would be roughly accurate.

23.   When Eberts and Hollenbeck refer to "the free lunch eligibility percentage," they mean the percentage eligible for free or reduced-price lunch.

24.   Nelson and Hollenbeck (2001) here are commenting on an earlier analysis of Arizona charter schools by Solmon, Paark, and Garcia (2001) that uses a methodology that is similar to that of Solmon and Goldschmidt (2004). We note that some charter school advocates have claimed that parent initiative would more likely be negatively related to test scores, because parents will be more likely to remove their children from regular public schools if the children are performing poorly. We know of no evidence that would confirm or refute this speculation.

25.   This analysis was performed by Roy using the database employed by Caroline Hoxby (2004a), which she supplied to him. We discuss the Hoxby (2004a and 2004b) studies using this database below, in Chapter 5.

Roy's sample for comparing rates of lunch eligibility excludes the charter schools (and their matched public schools) that report no students eligible. The excluded charter schools are not located in low-income areas relative to those included in his sample: the public schools that are matched to the excluded charter schools have lunch eligibility rates of 51%, less than the 64% rate in the regular public schools included in the sample.

26. KIPP is an acronym for the Knowledge Is Power Program.

27. Actually, the *USA Today*-cited comparison is silly, and doubtlessly understates the KIPP college-going advantage. Presumably, *USA Today* took the statistics from KIPP's own promotional material, which states that in New York City and Houston (combined), 76% of KIPP alumni are in college, compared to 48% of public high school seniors who matriculate to college (KIPP 2004). The statistical comparison is meaningless because, first, a comparison of KIPP middle school students and citywide high school seniors removes from the denominator of the citywide matriculation rate all those students who drop out between middle school and 12th grade; and second, the college-going rate in KIPP neighborhood regular public schools is probably much lower than the citywide rate. Although these inappropriate comparisons understate the KIPP advantage, they illustrate the fast-and-loose manner in which some charter school advocates discuss data in these public discussions.

28. It is even more of a stretch to argue for the superiority of KIPP by showing, as the Education Trust does in its Power Point presentations, that gains of KIPP students during the fifth grade surpass gains of all students nationwide during the fifth grade (Education Trust 2003, slide 19). In these comparisons, the Education Trust compares KIPP-D.C. gain scores from the fall of the fifth grade to the spring of the fifth grade to scores of all fifth-graders nationwide from the spring of fourth grade to the spring of fifth grade. This not only compares students who took tests at different times but who are different demographically.

  Test publishers usually provide standardized test norming data for three periods annually — fall, winter, and spring. The performance implications of raw test scores can vary considerably, depending on which norming period is used. KIPP's use of its beginning fifth-grade scores to compare with other schools' end-of-fourth-grade scores also cannot be properly evaluated without knowing to which national sample the fifth-grade scores were normed.

29. Included are all Bronx elementary schools within a two-mile radius of KIPP-Bronx Academy; schools in Manhattan were not included, even if they were within the two mile radius of KIPP.

  After reviewing Table 4 prior to publication, David Levin, superintendent of KIPP-Bronx, stated that the year (2002) for which we report these data was unusual, and that, in subsequent and prior years, entering KIPP students were more demographically typical of students in neighboring public schools. We chose the year 2002 for this table only because it was the only year for which both KIPP and neighboring public school data were available. We make no claim here that 2002 data for KIPP are representative of all years. David Levin also noted that the schools he had identified in column (c) as schools from which many students came to KIPP-Bronx were accurate for the early years of KIPP-Bronx, but may no longer be accurate. As the school has grown, Mr. Levin says he can no longer be sufficiently knowledgeable about the backgrounds of all students to be able to make a judgment about the schools from which they have predominantly come.

30. We were not able to attempt to interview every teacher who has referred students to KIPP or even to construct a randomly selected sample of them. We attempted to contact every teacher in a KIPP feeder school whose name and contact information we obtained. We identified teachers to interview by asking for referrals from local teachers' unions in

New York and Washington (we made multiple attempts to contact principals of regular public schools from which KIPP students came, but our messages were never returned) by sending out a mass e-mail inquiry to all members of the national 2002 cohort of the Teach for America program, and by seeking word-of-mouth referrals from graduate students at Teachers College, Columbia University, who had previously taught in urban schools from which KIPP students came, or who knew of such teachers. This resulted in the identification of 12 teachers who were willing and available to be interviewed. An interview with each of these was completed. Four of the interviewees were referred by teacher union representatives, two were graduate students at Teachers College, seven were Teach for America alumni, and one was referred by a Teachers College graduate student. Two of the teachers in this sample were currently working in KIPP Schools but had previously taught at regular public schools that referred children to KIPP.

Thus, our identification of teachers was opportunistic, but we have no reason to believe that our interview subjects were systematically different, in their referral strategies, from those we were not able to contact, especially because the responses were so similar among those we were able to contact. In soliciting potential interview subjects, we attempted to avoid telegraphing any policy orientation that might screen out potential subjects who would give contrary opinions. For example, the e-mail solicitation to Teach for America alumni said:

Dear TFA Alumni -

My name is Rebecca Jacobsen and I was a NYC 1996 [Teach for America] corps member. I taught 4th grade through 7th grade for 6 years in Harlem and then for another 2 years in Connecticut. I am now a graduate student at Teachers College, Columbia University, where I am conducting research on charter schools and their neighboring public schools.

I was hoping you would be willing to share with me any personal experiences you have had with students who transferred from your regular public school to a charter school (for example, a school like a KIPP Academy, or an Edison charter school, or an independent charter school), or from a charter school back to a regular public school. Of course, I do not need (or want) to know the names of individual students; I am only interested in their characteristics and your experiences with them or their parents. If you advised students to consider or not consider a transfer, either from a regular public to a charter school, or from a charter school back to a regular public school, or if you know of teachers in your school who gave such advice (even if the teachers were not corps members), I would be particularly interested in that.

If you would be willing to set up a short phone interview, please contact me either via email or phone with your phone number and some possible times to reach you.
Thank you for your help and I look forward to hearing from you.
    Rebecca Jacobsen
    rjj7@columbia.edu
    [telephone number provided]

A standardized interview questionnaire was utilized that avoided prompts that might stimulate specific answers. The authors will share the questionnaire with interested readers or other researchers.

31.   Some, but not all teachers we interviewed for this section did not wish to be identified by name in this report. For consistency, we have identified all by a teacher number.

The authors will use their best efforts to facilitate contact between these teachers and qualified researchers who wish to verify these interviews and who promise, where the teacher requests it, to respect the teacher's anonymity.

32. KIPP reports that, for the current (2004-05) school year, 53% of students were female at all 37 KIPP
middle/high schools currently in operation (Mancini 2005).

33. An interpretation, however, that the gender gap for urban students widened from fourth to eighth grade is still speculative. The trial urban assessment tested both fourth- and eighth-graders in 2003. To carefully support an interpretation of how the gender gap changed within a cohort as it aged from the fourth to eighth grade, we would need either fourth-grade scores from 1999 (to compare with eighth-grade scores in 2003), or eighth-grade scores from 2007 (to compare with fourth-grade scores in 2003). We cannot definitively support an interpretation that, if the eighth-grade gender gap for urban students was greater than the fourth-grade gender gap for urban students in 2003, this gap grew for urban students who were in fourth grade in 1999. However, such an interpretation is probable, because we know of no external factors that would make the relative gender performance for the urban cohort that was in the fourth grade in 2003 different from the relative gender performance of the urban cohort that was in the fourth grade in 1999.

For all black students nationwide, girls had NAEP eighth-grade reading scores in 1998 that were 14 scale points higher (nearly half a standard deviation) than boys' scores, a gap that was unchanged from the 14-point gender gap for black fourth-graders four years earlier, in 1994. The gaps in both years were statistically significant. In math, black eighth-grade boys had slightly higher NAEP scores than girls in 1996, a gender gap that had grown slightly from the fourth-grade gap in 1992. However, the gender gaps for black students in math were not statistically significant (Coley 2001, Figures 1 and 5).

34. In this respect, KIPP schools are similar to charter schools generally. The NAEP charter school study finds that 52% of charter school students are girls, while 49% of regular public school students are girls (NAEP 2005).

35. A selection process by lottery does not guarantee that charter school students will be representative of students in regular public schools, although charter school advocates often claim that this is the case. A lottery process only ensures that students who are admitted will be representative of those who choose to enter the lottery pool. Although Levin (2004a) has acknowledged that the lottery requirement prevents KIPP from selecting typical children in preference to the more advantaged, he and other KIPP supporters publicly claim that because "all of our kids come to us via lottery," KIPP is barred from making an effort to select more advantaged students, and that it is therefore a model for all schools serving disadvantaged children (Levin 2004b). The KIPP website states: "For the second consecutive year, KIPP ranks in the top 10% of all New York City public schools. What makes this fact even more impressive is that we continue to accept our students via lottery without regard to their prior academics or behavior" (KIPP b).

36. Thus, when we refer to KIPP's "apparent" effectiveness, we do not intend to suggest that the effectiveness is not real. Our use of the word "apparent" only arises because we have not independently investigated the progress KIPP students make once they are enrolled in KIPP, and so cannot ourselves confirm claims of effectiveness.

That KIPP student bodies are more advantaged than those of many regular public schools in low-income minority communities does not mean that KIPP's performance is not relatively better than that of these regular public schools. It does mean, however, that one cannot assess KIPP's relative performance by a simple comparison of test scores or even of gain scores. Whether KIPP's performance is better can be indicated only by a value-added (gain scores) analysis that also controls for self-selection — the fact that families choosing KIPP probably have parents who are more involved in their children's education than are parents in otherwise similar families who do not exercise such choice.

37. As noted above (see note 20 on page 149), 12 schools that had previously been classified as regular public schools were reclassified as charter schools.

38. Table 7 presents only means, not standard deviations. The NAEP web tool does allow computation of the standard deviation of test scores of all students in charter schools and of all students in regular public schools. These data show that the variation of test scores is similar for charter and for regular public schools. Unfortunately, the web tool does not allow the computation of such statistics for black or central city students or for other subgroups. These computations can be made when NCES makes the unrestricted NAEP data publicly available.

39. The NCES test for statistical significance found only one of these differences to be statistically significant — central city students who are not lunch-eligible scored lower in math than similar students in regular public schools. NCES notes, however, that even this difference should be treated with caution because of small sample size.

40. As to the authors of this report, two of us — Carnoy and Rothstein — have expressed skepticism in the past that charter schools are *the* solution to the ills of American public education, and have written that student achievement should not be assessed without demographic controls, but we have never opposed the limited establishment of charter schools as such (Benveniste, Carnoy, and Rothstein 2003; Rothstein 2004; Rothstein 2000). Jacobsen has not previously published her policy views on the subject. Prior to the publication of this report, Mishel wrote an on-line article (2004) commenting on reactions to the AFT's charter school NAEP report.

Of the researchers whose studies we cite below, Hanushek, Loveless, Hoxby, Solmon, Raymond, and Gronberg are on record as strong charter school advocates or are affiliated with institutions that advocate for more charter schools. Some of Ladd's previous work (e.g., Fiske and Ladd 2000) has been critical of charter schools. Witte (2004) states that charter schools are a way to provide opportunities for children who need them the most, but he believes it would be difficult to support a claim that achievement in charter schools is better or worse than in comparable schools because of the wide variety of chartering laws and the large number of at-risk students in charter schools. Bettinger (2004) has never taken a stance on the desirability of charter schools, and states that he would not do so, not only to preserve the credibility of his research but also to prevent the possibility that his research would be influenced by his stance. Similarly Randall Eberts (2004) states that neither he nor co-author Kevin Hollenbeck have taken a public position with respect to the desirability of charters, and their research on charters is financed solely by internal funds of the independent Upjohn Institute, which itself takes no position. Eberts notes, however, that Mr. Hollenbeck is a local school board member and past president of the Michigan Association of School Boards. Simeon Slovacek (2004) has been an education advisor to charter schools in California, has advocated the closure of charter schools that he considered corrupt, and believes that "it is only a matter of time before charters (after the bumpy startup years) surpass non charter public schools in academic performance." Professor Slovacek reports that his co-authors, Antony Kunnan and Hae Jin Kim, are testing experts who have never been involved in charter school advocacy or opposition. David Rogosa is a charter school advocate. We are not aware of Miron and Horn, Nelson, Risley, or Sass having taken previous public positions on the merits of charter schools.

41. We agree with the endorsement of "credible independent" journal reviews before publication of research on highly controversial topics, without suggesting that such reviews must or should be those conducted by academic "peer-reviewed" journals. Such reviews typically take much longer than is appropriate for policy-relevant research, and the "double-blind" process of such reviews, while having some advantages, also does not ensure that reviewers are without either positive or negative preconceptions regarding the subject of the research. Instead, we mean that, at a minimum, prior to publication it is desirable to submit such research to respected experts who are not predisposed to agree with the research conclusions and who can be expected, therefore, to call attention to possible weaknesses in the authors' arguments or methodologies.

During the controversy following the AFT's report on NAEP data, many charter school supporters argued that the AFT report should be dismissed for not having undergone a credible independent review, while at the same time these supporters endorsed research that had also not undergone credible independent reviews but where the conclusions were favorable to charter schools. This was true not only of the *New York Times* advertisement of August 25 (Exhibit A) by critics of the AFT report, but also of a statement distributed in the fall by the Charter School Leadership Council (CSLC 2004). This statement cites many studies that purportedly document the superiority of charter schools. Although it is possible that these studies were submitted to independent reviewers prior to publication, it is conventional in such cases to acknowledge and thank reviewers (even when they are anonymous), and none of these reports do so.

Among the studies cited by the Charter School Leadership Council is a report by the Charter Schools Development Center (CSDC), showing higher scores in 2001 for students in California charter schools that are five or more years old, than for students in California regular public schools (http://www.cacharterschools.org/charter.html). The CSDC is a charter school lobbying organization in Sacramento, California. Its report was done by staff members and does not acknowledge any credible independent reviewers. Its results showing higher scores for students in charter schools five or more years old presented these data for only one year and had no controls for race, social class differences, or grade of schooling between these older charter schools, regular public schools, and newer charter schools. It is hard to believe that any credible independent reviewer would have failed to object to such a poor study design. Because we do not consider this study to meet the most minimum threshold of scholarly credibility, it is not included in Table 8 or in the accompanying analysis.

The Economic Policy Institute usually (though not always) sends its proposed reports out for review to independent scholars prior to publication, and allocates time prior to publication for revisions based on the suggestions of these reviewers. The Economic Policy Institute is usually most careful about obtaining such independent reviews when studies deal with highly controversial issues, as in the case of the present volume where, as is our practice, we have acknowledged the reviewers by name (except in cases where the reviewers preferred to remain anonymous).

42.   As this book was going to press, the Charter School Leadership Council published its own review of state charter school studies (Hassel 2005). The studies analyzed in the council's review are almost identical to the studies listed in Table 8 or discussed in note 43, below. Hassel's analysis of these studies' methodologies, and his summary of their findings, concurs substantially with our own. However, Hassel makes no attempt to weigh the conclusions of these studies by the quality of the methodology used, although he notes that the studies vary greatly in quality. Because our analysis puts more emphasis on the quality of the studies in interpreting their results, we come to somewhat different interpretations about what the results mean for the performance of students in charter schools, although we differ little in our descriptions of what the studies actually find regarding student achievement.

43.   Studies of charter schools have also been done for some other states, but are not included in Table 8 either because we did not become aware of them until it was too late to include them in this publication, because they were not as comprehensive, or because they were missing too much data to be reliable. For example, an Ohio study of data from 2001-02 (LOEO 2003) found that, when charter school test scores, across grades and subjects, were compared with scores in matched regular public schools, there was no significant difference in about two-thirds of the individual matchings. In most of the remaining comparisons, traditional public schools did better but by small amounts. The study had no controls for student race, ethnicity, or socioeconomic background. Many of the charter schools (23 of 59) did not provide information for the study, although they were required by law to do so.

A study of New Jersey data (KPMG 2001) shows that charter schools have a higher proportion of black students than do regular public schools in students' districts of residence, and a lower percentage of Hispanics, but the share of lunch-eligible students in charter schools was lower (63%) than in their districts' regular public schools (70%). The study also finds that, from 1998-99, charter elementary school students made greater progress than students in their host districts' regular public schools in math but not in language arts or science; charter school eighth-graders made greater gains in language arts but not in math. However, these gain comparisons are based on a small sample of charter schools (nine elementary and six eighth grades) that had relevant test score data. None of the comparisons were corrected for socioeconomic background differences.

A recent study in New York (New York Board of Regents 2003) shows that the percentage of black students in charter schools is much higher than in host district public schools. Hispanic students are represented similarly in charter schools and in regular public schools statewide, but are underrepresented in New York City charter schools. The study asserts that the proportion of lunch-eligible students is higher in charter schools than in regular public schools statewide, but that, in large cities, the proportion of lunch-eligible students is similar in charter and in regular public schools (no data are provided). The study compares inter-cohort improvements in fourth-grade scores for 14 charter schools and regular public schools in their host districts; and it compares inter-cohort improvements in eighth-grade scores for five charter schools and regular public schools in their host districts. All but a few charter schools had greater improvements than regular public schools in the host districts. Nonetheless, more than half of these schools ended up with lower average scores than average scores of students in the host districts. The study makes no attempt to control for race, ethnicity, or lunch-eligibility in these comparisons.

The Georgia Department of Education produces an annual report on charter schools in that state. The most recent report (Georgia Department of Education 2004) shows that charter schools have a slightly higher percentage of black students than Georgia's regular public schools (41% to 38%), about the same percentage of Hispanic students (7%), but a much lower percentage of students eligible for free and reduced-price lunch (30% vs. 46%). Student test scores were about the same in charter and regular public primary and middle schools in 2004, and much lower in charter high schools. Improvement in test scores in 2002-04 (primary and middle grades combined) was the same for charter and regular public schools except in math, where it was higher in charter schools. Charter high schools had lower improvement in 2002-04, except in science. None of these aggregate results for Georgia control for race, ethnic, or socioeconomic differences in schools, nor make comparisons of charter schools with district averages. The Annual Report does compare student achievement results by grade for each individual charter school in the state (35 total charter schools in 2004) with its district average. The report also provides data on the demographic characteristics of each charter school, compared to nearby public schools. But the report does not use these data to analyze improvement in charter schools compared to regular public schools, adjusted for race, ethnicity, and social class.

44. See Nelson and Hollenbeck (2001) for a more detailed critique of how the authors of the Arizona study interpreted their results.

45. The differences were statistically significant at the 5% level.

46. Rogosa (2003) uses the same data as Raymond to show that socioeconomically disadvantaged students in charter schools made larger gains on the API, not, as Raymond found, smaller. He also finds that charter high schools made smaller gains than regular public schools for socioeconomically disadvantaged students, but they made much larger gains for socioeconomically disadvantaged students in schools with high percentages of socioeconomically disadvantaged students. These results are the opposite from Raymond's. One reason for this difference is that Raymond's regressions control for the previous year's API score. Rogosa argues: "[T]he inclusion of "Last Year's API" as a predictor in the multiple regressions Annual API Change Models (App. B) and Longitudinal API Change (App. C) effectively alters the outcome variable from amount of change to a *residualized change score*, a measure that researchers have been warned away from for over 20 years. Raymond's justification for including the prior API is: 'prior achievement is controlled (i.e. selection effect removed)'(p.22). Life would be nice if it were that easy. Residualized change scores address the question, How much would the school have changed if all schools had started out equal? rather than the answerable question, How much did the school improve?" (Rogosa 2003, 19).

47. Table 9 actually compares composite test scores in charter schools to composite test scores in all public schools, including charter schools. Because charter schools represent only 2% of all California public schools, it is reasonably accurate to interpret the table as comparing composite test scores in charters to composite test scores in regular public schools.

48. The charter schools included in the high socioeconomic disadvantage group had high socioeconomic disadvantage for three years. Because this group of charter schools does not include recent start-ups, the comparison of socioeconomically disadvantaged students in high socioeconomically disadvantaged schools should be most favorable to charter schools. Even so, students in charter schools do not perform as well — about 5% lower than the performance of regular public schools.

49. Rogosa (2002) has shown that Slovacek, Kunnan, and Kim made important school classification errors, and incorrectly defined the appropriate student population in schools with high concentrations of socially disadvantaged students. In a critique of the Slovacek, Kunnan, and Kim study, Rogosa (2002) corrected the dataset ("housecleaning notes," p. 5) and student social class categorization, and re-estimated API-type scores by grade, by grade/social class, and by grade/social class/size of school for 2001. (We call these "API-type" scores because the API itself is California's measure of *schoolwide* achievement.) Rogosa's results show that, generally, charter school students made lower gains than regular public school students, except in grades 9-11. This is also the case for socially disadvantaged students. In grades 2-6, a subset of socially disadvantaged students in charter schools with high concentrations of socially disadvantaged students made a 1 point higher gain than socially disadvantaged students in regular public schools with high concentrations of socially disadvantaged students. But in higher grades in schools with high concentrations of socially disadvantaged students, socially disadvantaged students in regular public schools had higher gains than such students in charter schools.

Estimation of gains at the secondary level is made more difficult because of increases in the number of charter schools and because of considerable variation in how well students do in different types of secondary charter schools, even those that use only classroom instruction. Zimmer et al. (2003) do not analyze gains. Yet, the data they present (Figure 3.4), using five years of test data (1997-98 to 2001-02) suggest that the higher gains in scores for charter schools reported by Rogosa at the secondary level may result from the addition of new, higher-scoring charter schools to the mix in 1999-2001. Zimmer et al.'s data show that start-up secondary charter schools that use only classroom instruction scored significantly higher than other schools, charter schools and regular public. If more of those schools entered the picture in 1999-2001, test scores could have risen even if existing secondary school charter schools made smaller gains than regular public schools in 1999-2001.

50. Bifulco and Ladd (2004) study students who switch from charter to public schools or vice-versa, and compare the relative test rankings of these students when in charter schools with their relative test rankings when in public schools. The Texas studies estimate the change in score in the year after the switch, whether that year was spent in a regular public or charter school, and compare this gain with that of other students in regular public and charter schools.

51. Bettinger (1999, 3) states: "I exploit exogenous variation created by Michigan's charter law, which allows state universities to approve charter schools. In particular, state universities where Governor Engler, an avid charter supporter, appoints the boards have approved 150 of Michigan's 170 charter schools. The proximity of a public school to one of these state universities can be used as an instrument for the likelihood that one or more charter schools were established nearby."

52. For 6% of all students nationwide to be in charter schools, charter schools would have to serve more than 3 million children, more than four times their current enrollment. For a minimum of 6% of students to be in charter schools in every district, many more than 3 million children would have to be served. This being the case, even if Hoxby is correct that a competition effect kicks in at 6%, this is not a practical approach to school reform for regular public schools in most school districts.

53. Hoxby's claim that 99% of elementary school students attending charter schools are included in her dataset is almost certainly exaggerated: in California (with about a fourth of all charter school students nationwide), many virtual, cyber-, and home schools file for waivers on state tests, and those students make up nearly one-third of the state's total charter school population. In Colorado as well, not all charter schools administer state tests.

54. Colorado, Delaware, and Wisconsin are important charter school states because they have at least 2% of their student enrollments in charter schools, but their absolute charter school student populations are not large.

55. Because the characteristics of the single nearest public school may not be a good proxy for the average characteristics of the entire neighborhood from which a charter school may draw many of its students, we find little or no contradiction between the analysis of Henig and MacDonald (2002), discussed on page 48, and this critique of the Hoxby methodology.

56. In previous work (Benveniste, Carnoy, and Rothstein 2003), two of us argued that market forces put pressure on private schools to be similar to public schools and put pressure on them not to develop unique niches that attract only some of the diverse clientele of public schools. This reasoning would apply equally to charter schools, and disputes the Finn-Manno-Vanourek claim that charter schools attract more homogeneous parents and students. In this paper, we do not repudiate our earlier claim. Our claim here is only that there is sufficient question about how the composition of charter schools and nearby regular public schools compare that Hoxby requires empirical evidence to support her assumption that the nearest public school is the best control for a charter school. Evidence from California (II and III) suggests that charter schools that are traditionally classroom-based seem to be similar in composition to nearby public schools, but charter schools that rely at least partly on out-of-classroom instruction (e.g., charters for home-schooled children and some alternative high school charters for students at high risk of dropping out) differ in composition from public schools.

57. Hoxby (2004) estimated that 8% more fourth-grade students achieved proficiency in Wisconsin's charter schools than in nearby public schools. Witte et al.'s (2004) results confirm that fourth-graders in Wisconsin charter schools are more likely to be proficient in various subjects than are fourth-graders in regular public schools, even when school average test scores are corrected for school racial composition and socioeconomic background. But both studies use school averages rather than individual student data, and this may be one reason why Hoxby's results agree with a specific state study for Wisconsin but do not agree with specific state studies elsewhere. School level averages corrected for race and socioeconomic composition differences among schools can yield different results from comparisons of the academic performance of groups of students of the same race or ethnicity in charter and regular public schools.

58. These conclusions appeared in a *Washington Post* (online) column by Jay Mathews, in which Mathews published, verbatim, an e-mail message he received from Nelson. Therefore, these conclusions are Nelson's, not Mathews' summary of them. The words and phrases in brackets are clarifications provided by Nelson (2004a, 2004b). Subsequent to publication of this e-mail message by Mathews, Nelson prepared a report (Nelson and

Miller 2004) describing, with technical detail, his findings regarding the Hoxby analysis. Although Nelson describes Hoxby's sample as including 100% of charter schools, Hoxby claims to have based her calculations on data from only 99% of charter schools. Both of these figures refer to elementary schools only where there were fourth-grade test scores. This small difference in description of the Hoxby sample is due to Hoxby's exclusion of schools where states do not report test results because too few students took the fourth-grade test.

59.   In response to a reporter's inquiry, Hoxby "attributed the mix-up to the difficulty of downloading data from different Web sites" (Dobbs 2004). (Dobbs, however, reports [2004] that Hoxby had reduced the advantage in math proficiency to 7.4%, not 13% as she reports in Hoxby [2004b], Table 4. Either Dobbs misunderstood Hoxby, or Hoxby has further revised her finding subsequent to the publication of Hoxby [2004b]).

60.   The Center for Education Reform report does not list all 2,874 schools by their date of founding. Therefore, we took the number of charter schools that might be considered mature enough to be subject to academic accountability as roughly equal to the number of charter schools already in existence three years before the center's report, or the fall of 1999. That number, after adjustment for closures for non-academic reasons, was approximately 1,500.

According to a Department of Education analysis:

> As of September 1999, more than 1,400 charter schools were in operation. Counting "branch schools" in Arizona, in which similar instructional programs are operated at several school sites under one charter, there were more than 1,600 charter school sites in operation....By the beginning of the 1999-2000 school year, 59 charter schools, nearly 4% of all charter schools ever opened, had closed (USDOE 2000).

61.   We do not know what steps the district takes, if any, to monitor the academic performance of these charter schools, and repeated efforts to contact district officials to inquire about this were unsuccessful. We note, however, that the Peach Springs website reports test scores for some charter schools and does not do so for others.

62.   The Thomas B. Fordham Institute report on charter school authorizers cites "resistance from parents and politicians" as the factor that makes it difficult to shut down a charter school when its students don't meet achievement goals (Palmer and Gau 2003, 15).

63.   Not all financial or mismanagement failures are corrupt. Some charter schools close after running out of funds because the charter operators were inexperienced and did not have the benefit of a district (bureaucratic) budget office. And not all charter school closures for mismanagement are effected by charter school authorizers. In many cases, authorizers do not take action until it is too late, or charter schools voluntarily close because their operators recognize that the management task is beyond their abilities.

64.   Indeed, in the case of public and private school comparisons, it is particularly important to have information on students' prior test scores (and not simply information on
scores of different cohorts of the same age in previous years) because more parents tend to
enroll younger children in private schools than older children. More children switch from
private to public schools as they get older than vice-versa. As a result, eighth-grade test
scores could be affected by whether some public school eighth-graders were better or
worse prepared in earlier grades in private schools.

65.   In his subsequent written statement, Martin R. West, one of the co-authors of the
Wall Street Journal op-ed that appeared on the day after the AFT report was released,
stated (Mathews 2004):
[O]ne cannot draw conclusions about how charter or private schools compare to traditional public schools, unless one compares two students with very similar backgrounds
— similar initial test scores, same race, similar parental education, similar place of residence, and more besides. Merely comparing groups of students sharing just one of these
characteristics, as the AFT has done, proves little, because all these factors together affect
student performance.

Bibliography

AFT (American Federation of Teachers) (F. Howard Nelson, Bella Rosenberg, and Nancy Van Meter). 2004a. *Charter School Achievement on the 2003 National Assessment of Educational Progress.* Washington, D.C.: American Federation of Teachers, August 20.

AFT (American Federation of Teachers). 2004b. "Charter Schools Underperforming, Results Repeatedly Delayed." http://www.aft.org/news/AFT_charterschools.htm, downloaded November 17, 2004.

Allen, Jeanne. 2004a. "Union Study of Charter Schools Fails in Accuracy." *Akron Beacon-Journal*, August 23. http://www.ohio.com/mld/ohio/news/editorial/9459736.htm, downloaded August 30, 2004.

Allen, Jeanne. 2004b. "Charter Schools Spark Reform." In Public Broadcasting System (PBS), *Closing the Achievement Gap.* http://www.pbs.org/closingtheachievementgap/debate_charter.html, downloaded November 22, 2004.

Allen, Jeanne. 2004c. Statement Made at Public Release of NCES NAEP Report by NAGB (the National Assessment Governing Board), Washington, D.C., December 15.

Allen, Jeanne, and Melanie Looney. 2002. *Charter School Closures: The Opportunity for Accountability.* Washington, D.C.: Center for Education Reform, October. http://www.edreform.com/_upload/closures.pdf, downloaded September 1, 2004.

Allen, Jeanne, and Anna Varghese Marcucio. 2004. *Charter School Laws Across the States: Ranking and Scorecard. 8th Edition. Strong Laws Produce Better Results. Special Report.* http://www.edreform.com/_upload/charter_school_laws.pdf, downloaded November 17, 2004.

Allington, Richard L., and Anne McGill-Franzen. 2003. "Summer Loss." *Phi Delta Kappan* 85(1): 68-75.

Angrist, Joshua D., and Alan B. Krueger. 1991. "Does Compulsory School Attendance Affect Schooling and Earnings?" *Quarterly Journal of Economics* 106 (4), November: 979–1014.

Angrist, Joshua D., and Alan B. Krueger. 2001. "Instrumental Variables and the Search for Identification: From Supply and Demand to Natural Experiments." *Journal of Economic Perspectives* 15 (4), Fall: 69-85.

Arenson, Karen W. 2004. "Math and Science Tests Find 4th and 8th Graders in U.S. Still Lag Many Peers." *New York Times*, December 15.

BAEO (Black Alliance for Educational Options). 2002. "Why Blacks Support Vouchers." Advertisement. http://www.schoolchoiceinfo.org/data/research/ACF8LSfcp.pdf, downloaded October 28, 2004.

Ballou, Dale. 2002. "Sizing Up Test Scores." *Education Next*, Summer.

BCPS (Baltimore City Public School System, Division of Research, Evaluation and Accountability). 2002. *Student Performance on the TerraNova: 1997-98 to 2001-2002. A Report Prepared for the Board of School Commissioners*, June 25. http://www.bcps.k12.md.us/Student_Performance/PDF/SA_Terranova_Comprehensive_Report_June2002.pdf, downloaded October 7, 2004.

Benveniste, Luis, Martin Carnoy, and Richard Rothstein. 2003. *All Else Equal. Are Public and Private Schools Different?* New York, N.Y.: RoutledgeFalmer.

Bettinger, Eric, 1999. "The Effects of Charter Schools on Charter Students and Public Schools." Teachers College, Columbia University, National Center for the Study of Privatization in Education. Occasional Paper No. 4, November. http://www.ncspe.org/publications_files/182_OP04.pdf (forthcoming in the *Economics of Education Review)*

Bettinger, Eric. 2004. Personal correspondence (with Martin Carnoy), November 29.

Bifulco, Robert, and Helen F. Ladd. 2004. "The Impacts of Charter Schools on Student Achievement: Evidence From North Carolina." Durham, N.C.: Sanford Public Policy Institute, Duke University.

Bruno, James, and Jo Ann Isken. 1996. "Inter and Intraschool Site Student Transiency: Practical and Theoretical Implications for Instructional Continuity at Inner-City Schools." *Journal of Research and Development in Education* 29(4): 239-252.

Buckley, Jack, Mark Schneider, and Yi Shang. 2004. "Are Charter School Students Harder to Educate? Evidence From Washington, D.C." Occasional Paper No. 96. National Center for the Study of Privatization in Education; http://ncspe.org/publications_files/OP96.pdf.

Burian-Fitzgerald, Marisa, Michael T. Luekens, and Gregory A. Strizek. 2004. "Less Red Tape or More Green Teachers: Charter School Autonomy and Teacher Qualifications." In Katrina E. Bulkley and Priscilla Wohlstetter, eds. *Taking Account of Charter Schools: What's Happened and What's Next?* New York, N.Y.: Teachers College Press.

Cannon, Mark. 2004. "NACSA Comments on NAEP's Charter School Test Data." Alexandria, Va.: NACSA (National Association of Charter School Authorizers), August 17. http://www.charterauthorizers.org/files/nacsa/Commentaries/nacsacomments-naep.pdf, downloaded September 1, 2004.

Cavanagh, Sean. 2004. "Greene Machine." *Education Week* 24 (7), October 13: 35-37.

CER (Center for Education Reform). 2003. *Important Information on DC School Reform Proposals.* July 17. http://www.edreform.com/_upload/fastfacts.pdf.

CER (Center for Education Reform). 2004a. "Charter School Evaluation Reported by *The New York Times* Fails to Meet Professional Standards." Paid Advertisement, *New York Times,* August 25.

CER (Center for Education Reform). 2004b. "Decade of Data Shows True Charter Success." http://www.edreform.com/index.cfm?fuseAction=document&documentID=1797&sectionID=127&NEWSYEAR=2004, downloaded August 29, 2004.

CER (Center for Education Reform). 2004c. "Decade of Data Shows True Charter School Success." Press Releases, CER Alert, August 12. http://www.edreform.com/index.cfm?fuseAction=document&documentID=1797&sectionID=55, downloaded November 20, 2004.

CER (Center for Education Reform). 2004d. "Another Piece of the Puzzle." *CER Newswire* 6 (36), September 14. http://www.edreform.com/index.cfm?fuseAction=document&documentID=1860&sectionID=72&NEWSYEAR=2004, downloaded October 31, 2004.

CER (Center for Education Reform). 2004e. "A Messenger for Education Reform" (holiday mailing), December.

Chubb, John. 2004. "Statement on AFT Study Story." Sent by e-mail to authors by Caleb Offley, Public Affairs, Hoover Institution's Koret Task Force on K-12 Education, October 29.

Coley, Richard J. 2001. *Differences in the Gender Gap: Comparisons Across Racial/Ethnic Groups in Education and Work.* Princeton, N.J.: Educational Testing Service, Policy Information Report, February

Colorado Department of Education. 2000. *1998 99 Colorado Charter Schools Evaluation Study.* Denver: Colorado Department of Education, January.

Colorado Department of Education. 2001. *The State of Charter Schools in Colorado, 1999-2000.* Denver: Colorado Department of Education, March.

Colorado Department of Education. 2002. *The State of Charter Schools in Colorado, 2000-2001.* Denver: Colorado Department of Education, April.

Colorado Department of Education. 2003. *The State of Charter Schools in Colorado, 2001-2002* Denver: Colorado Department of Education, March.

CSLC (Charter School Leadership Council). 2004. "The AFT and Charter Schools. A Study in Political Salesmanship." Statement distributed at "Charter Schools: Are They Working? A Century Foundation Forum on Issues for the Election and Beyond," Washington, D.C., National Press Club, October 27.

Davis, Michelle R. 2005. "Spellings to Face Senate Panel This Week." *Education Week* 24(16), January 5: 24, 26.

DCPS (District of Columbia Public Schools). *Academic Performance Database System: Summary Reports — Schools.* http://silicon.k12.dc.us/apds/APDSSummaryReports.asp, downloaded November 30, 2004.

Dillon, Sam, 2004. "Collapse of 60 Charter Schools Leaves Californians Scrambling." *New York Times*, September 17, A-1.

Dillon, Sam, and Diana Jean Schemo. 2004. "Charter Schools Fall Short in Public Schools Matchup." *New York Times*, November 23.

Dobbs, Michael. 2004. "Charter vs. Traditional. Two Types of D.C. Public School Are Not Easy to Compare." *Washington Post*, December 15, B01.

Doran, Harold C., and Darrel W. Drury. 2002. *Evaluating Success: KIPP Educational Program Evaluation.* Alexandria, Va.: New American Schools: Education Performance Network, October. http://www.naschools.org/uploadedfiles/Microsoft%20Word%20-%20KIPP%20Final%20Technical%20Report%2010.21.02%20_no%20embargo_.pdf, downloaded November 22, 2004.

Eberts, Randall W. 2004. Personal Correspondence (with Martin Carnoy), November 29.

Eberts, Randall W., and Kevin M. Hollenbeck. 2001. "An Examination of Student Achievement in Michigan Charter Schools." Staff Working Paper No. 01-68, March 9. Kalamazoo, Mich.: W.E. Upjohn Institute for Employment Research.

Eberts, Randall W., and Kevin M. Hollenbeck. 2002. "Impact of Charter School Attendance on Student Achievement in Michigan." Staff Working Paper No. 02-080. Kalamazoo, Mich.: W.E. Upjohn Institute for Employment Research.

Education Trust. 2003. "African American Achievement in America." Powerpoint presentation. http://www2.edtrust.org/NR/rdonlyres/47501795-973A-490A-9345-A03110A9651E/0/AchievementAfricanAmericanveryfinal.ppt, downloaded November 22, 2004.

Edwards, Leah (Administrative Assistant to the Superintendent, Peach Springs Unified School District). 2001. Affidavit. June 7.

ELC (Education Leaders Council). 2004. "ELC Refutes Recent 'Research' Regarding Student Achievement in Public Charter Schools." Washington, D.C.: Education Leaders Council, August 18.

Entwisle, Doris, and Karl L. Alexander. 1992. "Summer Setback: Race, Poverty, School Composition, and Mathematics Achievement in the First Two Years of School." *American Sociological Review* 57 (February): 72-84.

Farber, Peggy. 1998. "Boston: Renaissance Charter School." *American Prospect* 9(39), July 1.

Finn, Chester E., Jr. 2004a. "No August Break in Charter Land." *Education Gadfly* 4(30), August 19. http://www.edexcellence.net/foundation/gadfly/issue.cfm?id=159#1941, downloaded October 19, 2004.

Finn, Chester E., Jr. 2004b. "Defaming Charters." *New York Post Online*, August 19. http://www.nypost.com/postopinion/opedcolumnists/18765.htm, downloaded August 31, 2004.

Finn, Chester E., Jr. 2004c. "Slugging Back on Charters." *Education Gadfly* 4(31), August 26. http://www.edexcellence.net/foundation/gadfly/issue.cfm?id=160, downloaded December 22, 2004.

Finn, Chester E., Jr. 2004d. "Short Reviews of New Reports and Books." *Education Gadfly* 4(33), September 16. http://www.edexcellence.net/foundation/gadfly/issue.cfm?id=162, downloaded October 19, 2004.

Finn, Chester E., Jr. 2004e. Personal Correspondence (with Richard Rothstein), September 23.

Finn, Chester E., Jr. 2005. "The State of the Charter Movement, 2005." *Education Gadfly* 5(5), February 3. http://www.edexcellence.net/foundation/gadfly/index.cfm#2153, downloaded February 7, 2005.

Finn, Chester E., Jr., and Frederick E. Hess. 2004. "On Leaving No Child Behind." *Public Interest*, Fall: 35-56.

Finn, Chester E., Jr., Bruno V. Manno, and Gregg Vanourek. 2000. *Charter Schools in Action. Renewing Public Education.* Princeton, N.J.: Princeton University Press.

Finnigan, Kara, et al. (Nancy Adelman, Lee Anderson, Lynyonne Cotton, Mary Beth Donnelly, and Tiffany Price). 2004. *Evaluation of the Public Charter Schools Program. Final Report. 2004.* Doc No. 2004-08. U.S. Department of Education, Office of the Deputy Secretary.

Fiske, Edward B., and Helen F. Ladd. 2000. *When Schools Compete. A Cautionary Tale.* Washington, D.C.: Brookings Institution.

Flake, Floyd. 1999. "Drowning Kids in Failure." *New York Post*, March 20.

Flake, Floyd H. 2000. "School Choice in Urban Communities." *Policy Dialogue* 34, July. The Pioneer Network. http://www.pioneerinstitute.org/pdf/pdialg_34.pdf, downloaded August 31, 2004.

Flake, Floyd H. 2004. "Classes of Last Resort." *New York Times*, August 19.

Fuller, Howard. 2001. "Freedom to Learn Conference Keynote Remarks." Saint Paul, Minn., October 30. http://www.charterfriends.org/freedom.html#fuller, downloaded August 31, 2004.

Fuller, Howard, et al. 2003. "Educational Freedom and Urban America." *Cato Policy Report*, July/August. http://www.cato.org/pubs/policy_report/v25n4/education.pdf; downloaded September 2, 2004.

Fuller, Howard. 2004a. "Charter School Leadership Council Responds to Misleading *New York Times* Article." *EducationNews.org*, August 18. http://www.educationnews.org/ charter-school-leadership-counci.htm.

Fuller, Howard. 2004b. "Charter School Leadership Council Praises Hoxby's Study on Charter Achievement." September 12. http://groups.yahoo.com/group/ MarylandCharterSchoolNetwork/message/528, downloaded October 31, 2004.

GAO (U.S. General Accounting Office). 1994. *Elementary School Children: Many Change Schools Frequently, Harming Their Education*. GAO/HEHS-94-45. Washington, D.C.: author (ED 369-526).

Georgia Department of Education. 2004. *Charter Schools: 2003-2004 Georgia Charter Schools Program Annual Report*. Atlanta, Ga.: Department of Education.

Goldstein, Arnold (NAEP Project Officer for Scoring, Analysis and Reporting, National Center for Education Statistics). 2004. E-mail message (to Martin Carnoy), December 23.

Goldstein, Arnold (NAEP Project Officer for Scoring, Analysis and Reporting, National Center for Education Statistics). 2005. E-mail message (to Martin Carnoy), January 24.

Greene, Jay P. 2001. *High School Graduation Rates in the United States (with a forward by Kaleem Caire)*. Washington, D.C.: Black Alliance for Educational Options, and New York: Center for Civic Innovation at the Manhattan Institute, November.

Greene, Jay P., and Greg Forster. 2004. *The Teachability Index: Can Disadvantaged Children Learn?* Manhattan Institute, September 8.

Gronberg, Timothy J., and Dennis W. Jansen. 2001. *Navigating Newly Chartered Waters: An Analysis of Texas Charter School Performance*. Austin: Texas Public Policy Foundation. http://www.texaspolicy.com/pdf/2001-05-17-educ-newly.pdf, downloaded December 7, 2004.

Hahnel, Jesse (Senior Information Analyst, KIPP Foundation). 2005. E-mail message (to Richard Rothstein), February 2.

Hanushek, Eric A., John F. Kain, and Steven G. Rivkin. 2002. "The Impact of Charter Schools on Academic Achievement." December Revision. http://edpro.stanford.edu/ eah/papers/charters.aea.jan03.PDF, downloaded October 15, 2004.

Hanushek, Eric A., John F. Kain, and Steven G. Rivkin. 2004. "Disruption Versus Tiebout Improvement: The Costs and Benefits of Switching Schools." *Journal of Public Economics,* Summer.

Hassel, Bryan. 2005. *Charter School Achievement: What We Know.* Charter School Leadership Council, January. http://www.charterschoolleadershipcouncil.org/PDF/ Paper.pdf, downloaded February 1, 2005.

Hayasaki, Erika. 2004. "School's Out Too Early for 420 Kids on 2 Charter Campuses." *Los Angeles Times*, October 16, B-1.

Hayes, Sarah. 2004. Personal Interview (with Rebecca Jacobsen), September 7.

Hendrie, Carolyn, moderator. 2004. "Charter Schools: Policy and Practice." *Education Week Live Chat* (on-line discussion). November 18. http://www.edweek.org/chat/ transcript_11-18-2004.html, downloaded November 20, 2004.

Henig, Jeffrey R., Thomas T. Holyoke, Natalie Lacireno-Paquet, and Michele Moser. 2001. *Growing Pains: An Evaluation of Charter Schools in the District of Columbia; 1999-2000.* Washington, D.C.: Center for Washington Area Studies, George Washington University, February.

Henig, Jeffrey R., and Jason A. MacDonald. 2002. "Locational Decisions of Charter Schools: Probing the Market Metaphor." *Social Science Quarterly* 83(4), December: 962-80.

Hess, Frederick M. 2003. "The Case for Being Mean." *On the Issues.* American Enterprise Institute On-Line. http://www.aei.org/news/newsID.19614,filter./ news_detail.asp.

Howell, William G., and Paul E. Peterson. 2002. *The Education Gap. Vouchers and Urban Schools.* Washington, D.C.: Brookings Institution.

Howell, William G., Paul E. Peterson, and Martin R. West. 2004. "Dog Eats AFT Homework." *Wall Street Journal*, August 18.

Howell, William G., and Martin R. West. 2005. "Grey Lady Wheezing: The AFT Hoodwinks the *Times.*" *Education Next*, Winter (forthcoming), posted at: http:// www.ksg.harvard.edu/pepg/pdf/Howell_West_Charters.pdf, downloaded September 4, 2004.

Hoxby, Caroline M. 2001. "How School Choice Affects the Achievement of Public School Students." Prepared for Koret Task Force meeting on September 20-21, Hoover Institution, Stanford, Calif. http://post.economics.harvard.edu/faculty/hoxby/ papers.html, downloaded November 18, 2004.

Hoxby, Caroline M. 2003. "School Choice and School Competition: Evidence From the United States." *Swedish Economic Policy Review* 10:11-67. http://post.economics.harvard.edu/faculty/hoxby/papers.html, downloaded November 18, 2004.

Hoxby, Caroline M. 2004a. "A Straightforward Comparison of Charter Schools and Regular Public Schools in the United States." http://post.economics.harvard.edu/faculty/hoxby/papers/hoxbyallcharters.pdf, downloaded October 19, 2004.

Hoxby, Caroline M. 2004b. "Achievement in Charter Schools and Regular Public Schools in the United States: Understanding the Differences." December. http://www.ksg.harvard.edu/pepg/index.htm, downloaded December 15, 2004.

Hoxby, Caroline M., and Jonah E. Rockoff. 2004. "The Impact of Charter Schools on Student Achievement." May. http://post.economics.harvard.edu/faculty/hoxby/papers/hoxbyrockoffcharters.pdf, downloaded November 22, 2004.

Ifill, Gwen, interviewer. 2004. "Charter Schools." *A Newshour With Jim Lehrer Transcript*, August 18. http://www.pbs.org/newshour/bb/education/july-dec04/charter_8-18.html, downloaded October 28, 2004.

Jordison, Kristen (Executive Director, Arizona State Board for Charter Schools). 2004. Personal Interview (with Rebecca Jacobsen), December 3.

Kane, Thomas J., and Douglas O. Staiger. 2002. "The Promise and Pitfalls of Using Imprecise School Accountability Measures." *Journal of Economic Perspectives* 16(4), Fall.

Kerbow, David. 1996. "Patterns of Urban Student Mobility and Local School Reform." *Journal of Education for Students Placed at Risk* 12:147-69.

KIPP a (undated). *Highlights of the KIPP Academy.*

KIPP b. (undated). "Best scores EVER!!!! KIPP 8th Grade Ranks 17th in All of New York City in Reading and 20th in Math!!!" http://www.kippny.org/news/index.asp, downloaded January 20, 2005.

KIPP. 2004. "KIPP: KIPP Schools in Action. Student Achievement." http://www.kipp.org/studentachieve.cfm?pageid=nav1c, downloaded January 5, 2005.

KPMG. 2001. *The Evaluation of New Jersey's Charter School Program.* Trenton: New Jersey Department of Education, October 1.

Krueger, Alan, and Pei Zhu. 2004. "Another Look at the New York City School Voucher Experiment." *American Behavioral Scientist* 47(5), January.

Lacireno-Paquet, Natalie, Thomas T. Holyoke, Michele Moser, and Jeffrey R. Henig. 2002. "Creaming Versus Cropping: Charter School Enrollment Practices in Response to Market Incentives." *Educational Evaluation and Policy Analysis* 24(2), Summer: 145-58.

Ladd, Helen F., and Randall P. Walsh. 2002. "Implementing Value-Added Measures of School Effectiveness: Getting the Incentives Right." *Economics of Education Review* 21:1-17

Lee, Valerie E., and David T. Burkam. 2002. *Inequality at the Starting Gate.* Washington, D.C.: Economic Policy Institute.

Lerner, Robert. 2004. "Charter School Results." (Letter to the Editor.) *New York Times*, August 23.

Levin, David. 2004a. Personal interview (with Rebecca Jacobsen and Richard Rothstein), February 11.

Levin, David. 2004b. Presentation at public hearing of "Redesigning Schools for the 21st Century: Promising Innovations. Renewing Our Schools, Securing Our Future: A National Task Force on Public Education." New York, N.Y., December 10.

LOEO (Ohio Legislative Office of Education Oversight). 2003. *Community Schools in Ohio: Final Report on Student Performance, Parent Satisfaction, and Accountability.* Columbus, Ohio: LOEO.

Loveless, Thomas. 2003. "Chapter 3: Charter Schools, Achievement, Accountability, and the Role of Expertise." In *2003 Brown Center Report on American Education: How Well Are American Students Learning?* Washington, D.C.: Brookings Institution.

Mancini, Steve (Director of Public Affairs, KIPP Foundation). 2005. Letter to Richard Rothstein, February 9.

Mathews, Jay. 2002. "New School Paves Road to Success." *washingtonpost.com*, April 2. http://www.washingtonpost.com/ac2/wp-dyn?pagename=article&contentId= A51543-2002Apr2&notFound=true, downloaded November 20, 2004.

Mathews, Jay. 2004. "Are Charter Schools Any Good?" *washingtonpost.com*, October 28. http://www.washingtonpost.com/wp-dyn/articles/A18571-2004Nov2.html, downloaded November 12, 2004.

Miron, Gary, and Jerry Horn. 2002. *Evaluation of Connecticut Charter Schools and the Charter School Initiative.* Kalamazoo, Mich.: Evaluation Center, Western Michigan University (September). http://www.wmich.edu/evalctr/charter/ ct_cs_eval_final_report.pdf, downloaded December 7, 2004.

Miron, Gary, and Christopher Nelson. 2002. *What's Public About Charter Schools? Lessons Learned About Choice and Accountability.* Thousand Oaks, Calif.: Corwin Press.

Miron, Gary, Christopher Nelson, and John Risley. 2002. *Strengthening Pennsylvania's Charter School Reform: Findings From the Statewide Evaluation and Discussion of Relevant Policy Issues.* Kalamazoo, Mich.: Evaluation Center, Western Michigan University (October). http://www.wmich.edu/evalctr/charter/pa 5year/ 5_year_report_pa cs eval pdf, downloaded December 7, 2004.

Mishel, Lawrence. 2004. "Schoolhouse Schlock." *American Prospect On-Line Edition*, September 23. http://www.prospect.org/.

NAEP (National Center for Education Statistics, National Assessment of Educational Progress). 2004a. *The Nation's Report Card. Trial Urban District Assessment. Mathematics Highlights 2003. Results of the First NAEP 2003 Trial Urban District Assessment in Mathematics.* Washington, D.C.: NCES 2004-458.

NAEP (National Center for Education Statistics, National Assessment of Educational Progress). 2004b. *The Nation's Report Card. Trial Urban District Assessment. Reading Highlights 2003. Results of the NAEP 2003 Trial Urban District Assessment.* Washington, D.C.: NCES 2004-459.

NAEP (National Center for Education Statistics, National Assessment of Educational Progress). 2005. *The Nation's Report Card. America's Charter Schools: Results From the NAEP 2003 Pilot Study.* Washington, D.C.: NCES 2005-456.

NAGB (National Assessment Governing Board). 2002. "Reporting and Dissemination Committee, Report of May 17, 2002."

NCES (National Center for Education Statistics). 2004a. *Mini-Digest of Education Statistics 2003.* NCES 2005-017. Washington, D.C.: U.S. Department of Education, Institute of Education Sciences, October. http://nces.ed.gov/pubs2005/2005017.pdf, downloaded October 19, 2004.

NCES (National Center for Education Statistics). 2004b. *Issue Brief. The Summer After Kindergarten: Children's Activities and Library Use by Household Socioeconomic Status.* NCES 2004-037. Washington, D.C.: U.S. Department of Education, Institute of Education Sciences.

NCES (National Center for Education Statistics). 2004c. *Common Core of Data 2001-2002 and 2002-2003.* Washington, D.C.: U.S. Department of Education, Institute of Education Sciences. http://nces.ed.gov/ccd/search.asp.

Nelson, Christopher, and Kevin Hollenbeck. 2001. "Does Charter School Attendance Improve Test Scores? Comments and Reactions on the Arizona Achievement Study." Kalamazoo, Mich.: W.E. Upjohn Institute, Staff Working Paper No. 01-70, July.

Nelson, Christopher, and Gary Miron. 2002. *The Evaluation of the Illinois Charter School Reform.* Kalamazoo, Mich.: Evaluation Center, Western Michigan University.

Nelson, Howard. 2004a. E-mail message (to Larry Mishel), December 17.

Nelson, Howard. 2004b. E-mail message (to Richard Rothstein), December 19.

Nelson, F. Howard, and Tiffany Miller. 2004. "A Closer Look at Caroline Hoxby's *A Straightforward Comparison of Charter Schools and Regular Public Schools in the United States.*" Unpublished paper. Washington, D.C.: American Federation of Teachers.

Norris, Floyd. 2004. "U.S. Students Fare Badly in International Survey of Math Skills." *New York Times,* December 7.

New York Board of Regents. 2003. *Report to the Governor, the Temporary President of the Senate, and the Speaker of the Assembly on the Educational Effectiveness of the Charter School Approach in New York State*. http://www.emsc.nysed.gov/psc/5yearreport/fiveyearreport.htm.

NYCPS (New York City Public Schools). 2004. *2002-2003 Annual School Reports*. http://www.nycenet.edu/OurSchools/default.htm, downloaded September and October 2004.

NYSED (New York State Education Department). 2004. "KIPP Academy Charter School 2002-03. New York State Report Card (This page last updated on 03/17/2004)." http://www.emsc.nysed.gov/repcrdfall2003/schools/320700860820.html, downloaded November 23, 2004.

Paige, Rod. 2001a. "Remarks as Prepared for Delivery by U.S. Secretary of Education Rod Paige — Release of The Nation's Report Card — Fourth-Grade Reading 2000." National Center for Education Statistics, Washington, D.C., April 6. http://www.ed.gov/news/speeches/2001/04/010406.html, downloaded October 31, 2004.

Paige, Rod. 2001b. "Statement of U.S. Secretary of Education Rod Paige on President Bush's 2002 Education Budget Request, April 9, U.S. Department of Education Auditorium." Distributed by U.S. Department of Education list-serve, edinfo@inet.ed.gov, April 9.

Paige, Rod. 2001c. "Prepared Remarks of U.S. Secretary of Education Rod Paige. The Nation's Report Card — Mathematics 2000." National Center for Education Statistics, Washington, D.C., Aug 2. http://www.ed.gov/news/pressreleases/2001/08/08022001.html, downloaded October 31, 2004.

Paige, Rod. 2004. "Paige Issues Statement Regarding *New York Times* Article on Charter Schools." News Release, e-mail distribution from U.S. Department of Education, Office of Public Affairs, News Branch (Susan.Aspey@ed.gov), August 17.

Palmer, Louann Bierlein, and Rebecca Gau, 2003. *Charter School Authorizing: Are States Making the Grade?* Washington, D.C.: Thomas B. Fordham Institute, June.

Palmer, Louann Bierlein, and Rebecca Gau, 2005. "Charter School Authorizing: Policy Implications From a National Study." *Phi Delta Kappan* 86(5), January: 352-7.

Parker, Herman (Superintendent, Peach Springs Unified School District No. 8). 2001. "Ninety Day Revocation Letter to Real Life Charter School."

PPI (Progressive Policy Institute). 2002. "The AFT Charter Report: An Insult to Charter Schools." *21st Century Schools Project Bulletin* 2(15), July 23. http://www.ppionline.org/ppi_ci.cfm?knlgAreaID=110&subsecid=900001&contentid=250663, downloaded November 23, 2004.

Raudenbush, Steven W. 2004. *Schooling, Statistics, and Poverty: Can We Measure School Improvement?* Princeton, N.J.: Educational Testing Service, Policy Information Center, September.

Raymond, Margaret. 2003. *The Performance of California Charter Schools.* Stanford, Calif: CREDO, Hoover Institution (June). http://credo.stanford.edu/downloads/ca_chart_sch.pdf, downloaded December 7, 2004.

Reville, Paul, et al. (Celine Coggins, Jennifer Candon, and Dianne Le). 2004. "Massachuesetts Charter Schools and Their Feeder Districts: A Demographic Analysis." Boston, Mass.; Rennie Center for Education Research and Policy at MassINC. http://www.massinc.org/about/cerp/research/Charter_Schools/CharterSchoolReport.pdf.

Rice, Jennifer King. 2003. *Teacher Quality; Understanding the Effectiveness of Teacher Attributes.* Washington, D.C.: Economic Policy Institute

Rogosa, David. 2002. "A Further Examination of Student Progress in Charter Schools Using the California API." Stanford, Calif.: Stanford University, June. Unpublished paper. http://www-stat.stanford.edu/~rag/api/charter.pdf, downloaded November 22, 2004.

Rogosa, David. 2003. "Student Progress in California Charter Schools, 1999-2002." Stanford, Calif.: Stanford University, June. Unpublished paper. http://www-stat.stanford.edu/~rag/api/charter9902.pdf, downloaded November 22, 2004.

Rogosa, David. 2004. Tables of enrollment and API-type scores by race, ethnicity, and socioeconomic background, prepared for this report, using same database as in Rogosa 2003. Available from authors upon request.

Rosenbaum, Paul R., and Donald B. Rubin. 1983. "The Central Role of the Propensity Score in Observational Studies for Causal Effects." *Biometrika* 70(1), April: 41-55.

Rotherham, Andrew. 2004a. "*NYT* Update...And, Is the Education Sciences Reform Act Working?" *Eduwonk*, August 23. http://www.eduwonk.com/archives/2004_08_22_archive.html, downloaded October 6, 2004.

Rotherham, Andrew. 2004b. "Charter BS Interrupted...Was Fun While It Lasted!" *Eduwonk*, September 13. http://www.eduwonk.com/archives/2004_09_12_archive.html#109508339935615758, downloaded October 19, 2004.

Rothman, Robert. 2004a. "Telling Tales Out of Charter School." *Harvard Education Letter* 20(6), November/December: 1-2, 4.

Rothman, Robert. 2004b. "One Charter School's Formula for Success: Could It Work in a Large, Traditional Public School?" *Harvard Education Letter* 20(6), November/December: 3.

Rothstein, Richard. 2000. "Charter Schools in Action: Renewing Public Education" (Book Review). *American Prospect* 11(17), July 31.

Rothstein, Richard. 2004. *Class and Schools.* New York, N.Y.: Teachers College Press.

Rouse, Cecilia E. 1998. "Private School Vouchers and Student Achievement: An Evaluation of the Milwaukee Parental Choice Program. *Quarterly Journal of Economics* 113(2): 553-602.

Roy, Joydeep. 2005. *Comparing Charter Schools and Regular Public Schools: A Re-Examination of the Hoxby Study.* Washington, D.C.: Economic Policy Institute.

Rumberger, Russell, et al. 1999. "The Educational Consequences of Mobility for California Students and Schools." *PACE Policy Brief* 1(1), May. Berkeley, Calif.: Policy Analysis for California Education.

Sass, Tim. 2004. "Charter Schools and Student Achievement in Florida." Tallahassee: Department of Economics, Florida State University, October.

Schaeffler, Susan. 2004. Personal Interview (with Rebecca Jacobsen), September 7.

Schemo, Diana Jean. 2004. "Nation's Charter Schools Lagging Behind, U.S. Test Scores Reveal." *New York Times*, August 17.

Slovacek, Simeon. 2004. Personal Correspondence (with Martin Carnoy), November 29.

Slovacek, Simeon P., Antony J. Kunnan, and Hae-Jin Kim. 2002. "California Charter Schools Serving Low-SES Students: An Analysis of the Academic Performance Index." Los Angeles: Program Evaluation and Research Collaborative, Charter College of Education, California State University, March 11. http://www.calstatela.edu/academic/ccoe/c_perc/rpt1.pdf, downloaded November 22, 2004.

Soifer, Don. 2004. "AFT Attack on Charter Schools Meets Swift Response From Reformers." *School Reform News*, October 1. http://www.heartland.org/Article.cfm?artId=15698, downloaded October 28, 2004.

Solmon, Lewis C., and Pete Goldschmidt. 2004. "Comparison of Traditional Public Schools and Charter Schools on Retention, School Switching, and Achievement Growth." Phoenix, Ariz.: Goldwater Institute No. 192I, March 15.

Solmon, Lewis C., Kern Paark, and David Garcia. 2001. "Does Charter School Attendance Improve Test Scores? The Arizona Results." *Center for Educational Opportunity, The Goldwater Institute,* March 16. http://www.goldwaterinstitute.org/article.php/111.html.

Teacher1. 2004. Personal Interview (with Rebecca Jacobsen), October 17.

Teacher2. 2004. Personal Interview (with Rebecca Jacobsen), October 18.

Teacher3. 2004. Personal Interview (with Rebecca Jacobsen), November 22.

Teacher4. 2004. Personal Interview (with Rebecca Jacobsen), November 15.

Teacher5. 2004. Personal Interview (with Rebecca Jacobsen), November 10.

Teacher6. 2004. Personal Interview (with Rebecca Jacobsen), November 11.

Teacher7. 2004. Personal Interview (with Rebecca Jacobsen), December 2.

Thernstrom, Abigail, and Stephan Thernstrom. 2003. *No Excuses. Closing the Racial Gap in Learning*. New York, N.Y.: Simon and Schuster.

USA Today. 2005. "Charters: Success or Failure?" January 4.

USDOE (United States Department of Education). 2000. *The State of Charter Schools 2000 — Fourth-Year Report, January 2000*. http://www.ed.gov/pubs/charter4thyear/a.html, downloaded September 1, 2004.

USDOE (United States Department of Education). 2004a. *PISA Results Show Need for High School Reform. U.S. 15-Year-Olds Outperformed by Other Nations in Mathematics, Problem-Solving*. Press Release, December 6. http://www.ed.gov/news/pressreleases/2004/12/12062004a.html, downloaded December 15, 2004.

USDOE (United States Department of Education). 2004b. *U.S. Students Show Improvement in International Mathematics and Science Assessment. U.S. Fourth- and Eighth-Graders Score Well Above International Average in 46-Nation TIMSS Study*. Press Release, December 14. http://www.ed.gov/news/pressreleases/2004/12/12142004.html, downloaded December 15, 2004.

Wells, Amy Stuart, et al. 1998. *Beyond the Rhetoric of Charter School Reform: A Study of Ten California School Districts*. Los Angeles, Calif.: UCLA Charter School Study. http://www.gseis.ucla.edu/docs/charter.PDF, downloaded November 17, 2004.

Witte, John F. 2004. Personal Correspondence (with Martin Carnoy), November 27.

Witte, John F., et al. (David L. Weimer, Paul A. Schlomer, and Arnold F. Shober). 2004. "The Performance of Charter Schools in Wisconsin." August. Madison: Department of Political Science, Robert LaFollette School of Public Affairs, University of Wisconsin. http://www.lafollette.wisc.edu/wcss/papers.html#per04.

Zimmer, Ron, Richard Buddin, Derrick Chau, Brian Gill, Cassandra Guarino, Laura Hamilton, Cathy Krop, Dan McCaffrey, Melinda Sandler, and Dominic Brewer. 2003. *Charter School Operations and Performance: Evidence From California*. Santa Monica, Calif.: Rand Corporation, MR-1700-EDU.

Acknowledgments

Although each co-author of this report took initial responsibility for different sections of it, all four have reviewed and revised the entire book and take responsibility for the whole. Readers with comments or questions about this book's analysis or conclusions may communicate with any of the authors:

Martin Carnoy: carnoy@stanford.edu
Rebecca Jacobsen: rjj7@columbia.edu
Lawrence Mishel: lmishel@epinet.org
Richard Rothstein: rr2159@columbia.edu

We benefited from the advice of many colleagues who are too numerous to mention here. But we make special note of the following: upon completion of a first draft of the manuscript of this book, we received a fine internal review from Joydeep Roy at the Economic Policy Institute. We extend our appreciation to him. We then asked a number of outside experts to review the manuscript and make criticisms and suggestions for revision. The subsequent revisions were substantial, and these reviewers may be surprised at the extent to which this book has changed (improved, we hope) from the first draft. We are grateful to the following policy experts and scholars who served as reviewers: Clive Belfield, Christopher Cross, David Figlio, Gary Miron (who reviewed chapters 4 and 5), Jeffrey Henig, Luis Huerta, Steven Raudenbush, Richard Shavelson, and John Witte.

David Rogosa provided unique data analyses for our use in chapters 4 and 5, and we are indebted to him for this generosity.

Patrick Watson, our copy editor, did his usual fine job in clarifying our language to ensure that this volume actually says what we intended.

Upon completion of the first draft, we requested a meeting with leaders of KIPP Schools, because we use KIPP in this book to illustrate some broader points about charter schools generally. David Levin, co-founder and superintendent of KIPP-New York, and Steve Mancini, KIPP public affairs director, graciously agreed to meet with us and to read and critique sections of the manuscript relating to KIPP. As they knew, in advance, that we would probably not be presenting data about KIPP in the way they might prefer it be presented, their willingness to meet with us and to advise us about how the presentation could be corrected and improved was extraordinary in its magnanimity. We are very appreciative of their assistance. While we made some changes in the text based on their advice, we rejected other changes they proposed. While we stand by the accuracy of our reporting about KIPP, the participation of KIPP officials in this process does not in any way imply that they agree with how KIPP is presented in this volume. Based on our discussions, we expect that KIPP will publicly disagree with some of our conclusions. We welcome this public discussion and believe that policy debates can only be enhanced by reasoned debate of the issues we have raised.

Likewise, we are grateful to teachers whom we interviewed about their reasons for referring children to charter schools in general and to KIPP in particular. While most of them gave us permission to use their names, we have identified all by a teacher number for reasons of consistency. It is self-evident that these teachers think highly of KIPP; that, after all, is the reason they refer children to it. While we use the information they provided to us to show that KIPP students are probably not fully representative of their neighborhoods, we would not be surprised if some of our interviewees were chagrined that evidence regarding their referrals tends to discredit commonplace claims about the representativeness of KIPP students. To these teachers we can only say that we are confident that we have presented accurately and fairly the information they gave to us, and welcome their participation in these discussions should they disagree with how we have interpreted the policy implications of their experiences.

Of course, we remain solely responsible for errors of fact and interpretation that remain in this book, despite the best efforts of our reviewers and, in the case of KIPP, our subjects, to correct them. In the case of some reviewers, although we may have adopted many of the suggestions that they made, this does not imply that they agree with any part of the book or with its overall themes. We certainly hope that we persuaded them, but do not assume that this is the case.

About EPI

The Economic Policy Institute was founded in 1986 to widen the debate about policies to achieve healthy economic growth, prosperity, and opportunity.

In the United States today, inequality in wealth, wages, and income remains historically high. Expanding global competition, changes in the nature of work, and rapid technological advances are altering economic reality. Yet many of our policies, attitudes, and institutions are based on assumptions that no longer reflect real world conditions.

With the support of leaders from labor, business, and the foundation world, the Institute has sponsored research and public discussion of a wide variety of topics: trade and fiscal policies; trends in wages, incomes, and prices; education; the causes of the productivity slowdown; labor market problems; rural and urban policies; inflation; state-level economic development strategies; comparative international economic performance; and studies of the overall health of the U.S. manufacturing sector and of specific key industries.

The Institute works with a growing network of innovative economists and other social science researchers in universities and research centers in the U.S. and abroad who are willing to go beyond the conventional wisdom in considering strategies for public policy.

About Teachers College Press

For over a century, Teachers College Press (the university press of Teachers College, Columbia University) has been committed to addressing the ideas that matter most to educators. Teachers College Press provides authoritative and practical resources for all participants in the education process, including teachers, teacher educators, researchers, academics, administrators, school board members, policymakers, parents, and students. Teachers College Press publishes many cutting-edge, critically acclaimed books, videos, and CD-ROMs in the subject areas of educational leadership and policy, language and literacy, early childhood education, math and science, social studies, teacher education, school reform, multicultural education, urban education, sociology, and much more.

Titles of particular interest to educators from the Economic Policy Institute

The following books can be ordered on the EPI website, www.epinet.org.

Teacher Quality: Understanding the Effectiveness of Teacher Attributes
Jennifer King Rice

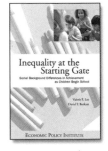

Teacher quality is the single most important school-related factor influencing student success. In this study Jennifer King Rice examines the body of research to draw conclusions about which attributes make teachers most effective, with a focus on aspects of teacher quality that can be translated into policy recommendations and incorporated into teaching practice.

Inequality at the Starting Gate: Social Background Differences in Achievement as Children Begin School
Valerie E. Lee and David T. Burkam

Inequality at the Starting Gate examines the learning gap between rich and poor children when they enter kindergarten. This study, by two education experts from the University of Michigan, analyzes U.S. Education Department data on 16,000 kindergartners nationwide, showing the direct link between student achievement gaps and socioeconomic status. The report finds that impoverished children lag behind their peers in reading and math skills even before they start school. The book also reveals how a lack of resources and opportunities can cause lasting academic damage to some children, underscoring the need for earlier and more comprehensive efforts to prepare children to succeed in school.

Smart Money:
Education and Economic Development
William Schweke

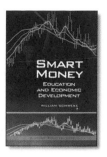

Strong economies compete on the basis of high value, not solely low cost. The most forward-thinking approach to increasing U.S. competitiveness is to equip today's and tomorrow's citizens with the skills and attitudes needed for economic and civic success in an increasingly knowledge-based economy. Existing research shows that a nation that invests in education generates real, quantifiable results. For a better understanding of why money spent wisely on education pays off not only for workers, but for communities and businesses, read *Smart Money*.

How Does Teacher Pay Compare?
Methodological Challenges and Answers
Sylvia A. Allegretto, Sean P. Corcoran,
& Lawrence Mishel

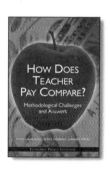

Recent claims have suggested that teachers are well compensated when work hours, weeks of work, or benefits packages are taken into account. In fact, teacher compensation lags that of workers with similar education and experience, as well as that of workers with comparable skill requirements. Incorporating benefits into the analysis does not alter the general picture—teachers remain at a substantial wage/pay disadvantage that has eroded considerably in the last 10 years. *How Does Teacher Pay Compare?* reviews recent analyses of relative teacher compensation and provides a detailed analysis of trends in the relative weekly pay of elementary and secondary school teachers.

School Choice: Examining the Evidence
Edith Rasell & Richard Rothstein, editors
Opinions about school choice have been formed largely on the basis of theoretical assertions that it offers the answer for the problems of public education. But researchers studying actual programs find that choice of schools neither raises student achievement nor enhances equality of opportunity, and may exacerbate racial segregation and socioeconomic stratification.

Exceptional Returns
Economic, Fiscal, and Social Benefits of Investment in Early Childhood Development
Robert G. Lynch

The problems for children and society that result from childhood poverty cry out for effective policy solutions. There is a strong consensus among the experts who have studied high-quality early childhood development (ECD) programs that these programs have significant payoffs. *Exceptional Returns: Economic, Fiscal, and Social Benefits of Investment in Early Childhood Development*, by EPI research associate Robert G. Lynch, demonstrates, for the first time, that providing all 20% of the nations three- and four-year-old children who live in poverty with a high-quality ECD program would have a substantial payoff for governments and taxpayers in the future.

Market-Based Reforms in Urban Education
Helen F. Ladd

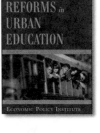

In the debate over reforming urban education, the issues surrounding market-based approaches — charter schools, vouchers, public school choice — are complex. This EPI book examines the extensive but disparate evidence to help determine whether these reforms promote the public interest and translate well into the provision of compulsory education.

The Class Size Debate
Lawrence Mishel and Richard Rothstein, editors;
Alan B. Krueger, Eric A. Hanushek,
and Jennifer King Rice, contributors

Two eminent economists — Professors Krueger and Hanushek — debate the merits of smaller class size and the research methods used to gauge the efficacy of this education reform measure. Professor Rice synthesizes their arguments and highlights the points of agreement in their different perspectives.

School Vouchers:
Examining the Evidence
Martin Carnoy
Does a voucher threat make schools try harder? A recent Florida study of this education reform approach
said yes, but three analyses that replicate its methods
show there's no basis for that claim.

Can Public Schools Learn From Private Schools?
Case Studies in the Public & Private Sectors
Richard Rothstein, Martin Carnoy, and Luis Benveniste
Rothstein, Carnoy, and Benveniste report on case studies of eight public
and eight private schools, which they conducted to determine whether
there are any identifiable and transferable private school practices that
public schools can adopt in order to improve student outcomes. The evidence from interviews with teachers, administrators, and parents yields a
surprising answer, one that should inform our policy debates about school
choice, vouchers, public school funding, and other education issues.

Class and Schools:
Using Social, Economic, and Educational Reform
to Close the Black-White Achievement Gap
Richard Rothstein
At the 50th anniversary of the U.S. Supreme Court's
landmark Brown v. Board of Education ruling, the stub-
born achievement gap between black and white students is a key measure of our country's failure to

achieve true equality. Federal and state officials are currently pursuing
tougher accountability and other reforms at the school level to address
this problem. In making schools their sole focus, however, these policy
makers are neglecting an area that is vital to narrowing the achievement
gap: social class differences that affect learning. This book, co-published
by the Economic Policy Institute and Teachers College, Columbia University, shows that social class differences in health care quality and
access, nutrition, childrearing styles, housing quality and stability, parental occupation and aspirations, and even exposure to environmental
toxins, play a significant part in how well children learn and ultimately
succeed.

Titles of particular interest to educators from Teachers College Press

Bringing Equity Back: Research for a New Era in American Educational Policy
Edited by Janice Petrovich and Amy Stuart Wells
Foreword by Alison Bernstein
Afterword by Wendy Puriefoy

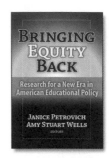

Well-known scholars present new analyses of the current status of past reforms, such as **desegregation**, **ability tracking**, and **affirmative action**, and investigate more recent reforms, such **high-stakes testing**, **vouchers**, and **charter schools**. They also examine historical, economic, and political conditions that generate inequalities in educational opportunity.
Contributors include: Mark Berends, Martin Carnoy, Marilyn Gittell, George Madaus, Roslyn Arlin Mickelson, Jeannie Oakes, Harry P. Pachón, and Michael A. Rebell.

School Choice and Diversity:
What the Evidence Says
Edited by Janelle Scott
Foreword by Henry Levin

This collection of essays will help readers to disentangle the complex relationship between school choice and student diversity in the post-*Brown* era. Features the views of the most prominent researchers of school choice reforms in the United States.
Contributors: Robert Fairlie, Hamilton Lankford, James Wyckoff, Jay Greene, John Yun, Sean Reardon, Amy Stuart Wells, Robert Crain, Carol Ascher, Nathalis Wamba, Kevin Welner, Kenneth Howe, Amanda Datnow, Lea Hubbard, Betsy Woody, Roslyn Arlin Mickelson

Letters to the Next President: What We Can Do About the Real Crisis in Public Education
Edited by Carl Glickman
Prologue by Bill Cosby

This impressive collection of more than thirty letters speaks to the critical issues in public education, such as: guaranteeing higher standards with comprehensive assessments; allocating equitable resources with responsible local control; attracting and retaining good teachers; improving school choice and the promise of small schools; providing for universal high quality early childhood education, and ensuring a rich, academically sound and engaging curriculum for all students.

Contributors: Sylvia Bruni • Jane Butters • Louis Casagrande • Bill Cosby • Linda Darling-Hammond • Lisa Delpit • Rosa Fernández • Michelle Fine, April Burns, & María Elena Torre • U.S. Senator John Glenn & Leslie F. Hergert • John I. Goodlad • Maxine Greene • Karen Hale Hankins • Asa G. Hilliard III• Richard Ingersoll • Jacqueline Jordan Irvine • U.S. Senator Jim Jeffords • Lilian Katz • Reynold Levy • William J. Mathis • Deborah Meier • Edward C. Montgomery • Navajo Students with Mark Sorensen • Pedro Noguera • Jeannie Oakes • Martin Lipton • Arturo Pacheco • W. James Popham • Vance Rawles • Ken Rolling & Sandra Halladey • Sophie Sa • Ted Sizer •Thomas Sobol • Pam Solo • Rachel Tompkins • The late U.S. Senator Paul Wellstone • George Wood

City Schools and the American Dream: Reclaiming the Promise of Public Education
Pedro Noguera

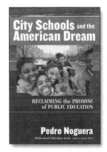

What will it take for urban schools to achieve the kind of academic performance required by new state and national educational standards? How can classroom teachers in city schools help to close the achievement gap? Drawing on extensive research performed in San Francisco, Oakland, Berkeley, and Richmond, Noguera demonstrates how school and student achievement is influenced by social forces such as demographic change, poverty, drug trafficking, violence, and social inequity. Readers get a detailed glimpse into the lives of teachers and students working "against the odds" to succeed.

**Charter Schools: Another Flawed
Educational Reform?**
Seymour B. Sarason

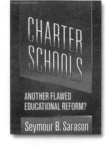

The potential significance of charter schools is great.
Yet Professor Sarason reluctantly concludes that most
charter schools will fail or fall far short of their goals
and only a small number will be considered successful. If future charter schools are to exploit this potential, their supporters and creators should seriously study the findings
and recommendations in this book.

**Whatever It Takes:
Transforming American Schools—
The Project GRAD Story**
Holly Holland
Foreword by Donna Peterson

This volume examines one of the largest and most
promising urban school reform initiatives, Project
GRAD (Graduation Really Achieves Dreams) —an extraordinarily successful program that has been adapted to many locations across the United States. This compelling story offers concrete
solutions to the chronic problems of urban schools struggling with poverty and the incessant demands of state and federal mandates.